TEACHING GUIDE

PURSUING **SPIRITUAL** AUTHENTICITY

TEACHING GUIDE

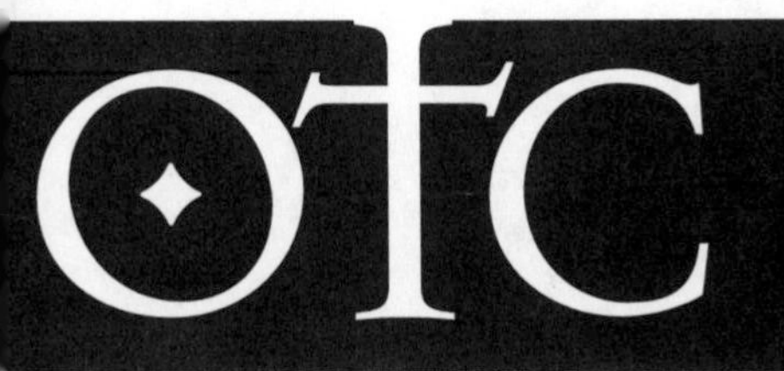

OLD TESTAMENT
CHALLENGE
4

PURSUING SPIRITUAL AUTHENTICITY

LIFE-CHANGING WORDS FROM THE PROPHETS

JOHN ORTBERG
WITH KEVIN & SHERRY HARNEY

GRAND RAPIDS, MICHIGAN 49530 USA

WILLOW
Willow Creek Resources

We want to hear from you. Please send your comments about this book to us in care of zreview@zondervan.com. Thank you.

ZONDERVAN™

Old Testament Challenge Volume 4: Pursuing Spiritual Authenticity Teaching Guide

Requests for information should be addressed to:

Zondervan, *Grand Rapids, Michigan 49530*

ISBN 0-310-25143-5

Interior design by Sharon VanLoozenoord

Interior composition by Tracey Moran

Printed in the United States of America

04 05 06 07 08 09 /❖ ML/ 10 9 8 7 6 5 4 3 2 1

CONTENTS

OTC

Introduction

The Old Testament Challenge (OTC) is designed to foster spiritual formation and growth on three distinct levels (congregation-wide, small group, and individual). The first level of learning is with the full community of God's people. This teaching resource can be used in the setting of a worship service or in a large class. The primary reason these materials were developed was for use in a worship service, but there could also be some application of these materials in a larger class setting.

This teaching resource is designed to give teachers a wealth of ideas as they prepare to bring a message from God's Word. These materials have been designed to provide a large pool of information on the text and ideas for preaching. From these materials, the teacher can shape and form a message that fits the congregation he or she serves. As you will discover when you begin to dig into the teaching resources, there are far more source materials and ideas than can be incorporated in a normal sermon or teaching session. You will each need to decide what materials best fit your situation, add your own personal illustrations and teaching ideas, and then form a message that fits your congregation and personal teaching style.

These materials have intentionally been developed on two levels. First, John Ortberg wrote the initial messages and preached them at Willow Creek Community Church. John developed these messages to teach them at the New Community Believers' Services. You will find an audiotape or CD of these messages in each of the four OTC kits. You will also notice that there were a few guest preachers who took part in the OTC teaching at Willow Creek.

The materials and resources from the OTC were then adapted for a second-generation OTC church, Corinth Church in Grand Rapids, Michigan. Kevin Harney continued the process of developing and expanding the materials as he preached the messages in the Sunday morning services at Corinth Church. New illustrations, creative message ideas, Power Point presentations, Frequently Asked Question sheets (FAQs), and other study materials were added and the messages were expanded. Although John Ortberg was the primary writer/teacher at Willow Creek and Kevin Harney the primary writer/teacher at Corinth Church, a whole team of teachers, leaders, and editors have partnered together to develop and create this teaching resource.

What makes the teaching resource for the OTC so unique are the many different tools offered to the teacher in this Old Testament Challenge kit. When you open the teacher's resource, you will find the following categories of material in various combinations:

- The Heart of the Message
- The Heart of the Messenger
- Creative Message Idea
- Historical Context
- Illustration
- Interpretive Insight
- Life Application
- Narrative on Life
- Narrative on the Text
- New Testament Connection
- On the Lighter Side
- Pause for Prayer
- Pause for Reflection
- Quotable Quote
- Significant Scripture
- Word Study

It is important to note that some of the teaching resources listed above will appear in every study (for example, The Heart of the Message, The Heart of the Messenger, and Interpretive Insight). Some of the other resources might appear in one message but not in another. The sixteen various components of the OTC messages contained in this teaching guide are defined in the pages that follow. As you review what each of these teaching tools offers, you will begin to get a sense for the depth and breadth of what is offered in each of the OTC message resources.

The Heart of the Message

This is a brief description of the heartbeat or central theme of *the entire message*. Each message will begin with a short section to help the teacher gain a sense of the core idea or ideas being communicated in each OTC message.

The Heart of the Messenger

Teachers and preachers can't communicate with passion and clarity until their hearts have been touched and impacted by the truth of God's Word. This section of the teacher's resource will give some direction for how each teacher can begin to prepare to study and open his or her heart to what the Holy Spirit wants to say. One of the goals of the Old Testament Challenge is to help teachers move forward in their own journey of faith. We believe the process of self-examination, deep learning, and personal growth that will be experienced while leading the OTC can be life-changing! This section will usually include a few questions for personal reflection as the teacher prepares to bring the OTC message.

Creative Message Idea

This section of the OTC teaching resource will offer a broad variety of ideas a teacher can use to bring a biblical point home with power. This section will include video pieces developed specifically for OTC messages. It will also include a number of ideas for using props or visual aids to communicate a relevant biblical truth. Some of the creative message ideas will help the teacher move worshipers to respond or interact during the message. We can't begin to cover all the creative ideas that have been developed to bring the message of the Old Testament alive, but if you take a few moments and skim through this OTC teacher's resource, you will begin to get a sense of the kinds of creative ideas that are available for a teacher or preacher. In an effort to make these ideas user-friendly, we have listed everything that is needed to naturally incorporate each creative idea into the message. Each of these ideas has been used effectively at Willow Creek or Corinth Church, or both, but we encourage you to decide which ones will connect in your particular context.

Historical Context

Throughout the teacher's resource you will find helpful notes on the historical context of certain passages. There are a number of texts we will study in the OTC that make much more sense when we have an understanding of the culture and the world of the Old Testament. The Historical Context notes are provided to help you teach about this kind of background information. These notes are not designed to be highly academic observations but are intended to help the teacher make natural observations about culture and customs that will bring the message of the Old Testament alive.

Illustration

Jesus was a master storyteller. He used word pictures to illustrate much of what he taught. In the teacher's resource we have provided many ideas for illustrating core Old Testament ideas. Sometimes these illustrations can be read just as they are printed in this teacher's guide. At other times, you as the teacher will be given ideas or direction on developing an illustration out of your own life or ministry. You must decide whether an illustration fits in your setting. Even if a particular illustration does not fit in your context, it might spark some ideas for an illustration that does.

Interpretive Insight

A huge part of teaching the Bible is doing interpretive work. We have provided solid biblical interpretation that can function as the backbone of each OTC message. This does not mean that the teacher should avoid additional study, but it does offer a great starting point. The major texts being used in each message will have a brief, or sometimes extended, section of biblical interpretation provided in the teacher's resource guide.

Life Application

In the book of James we read these words, "Do not merely listen to the word, and so deceive yourselves. Do what it says" (James 1:22). Any study of God's Word that is going to have life-changing power must include application. In each OTC message you will find ideas for life application. Sometimes these ideas are specific. They will give detailed instruction on concrete ways a congregation can respond to God's Word. At other times these applications will be broad, intended to encourage individual reflection upon a specific area of life. In these cases, the specific application will come as the Holy Spirit speaks to the heart of each person and shows where change needs to take place.

Narrative on Life

Occasionally telling a story from everyday life is the best way to bring a biblical truth home to the listeners. In this OTC teacher's guide we have captured some great examples of life narratives that speak powerfully. These can be used as they are found in the teacher's guide, or you can retell them in your own words.

Narrative on the Text

One of the unique gifts John Ortberg has as a preacher is the ability to tell a familiar biblical story in a fresh narrative form. This retelling of the story, including some natural commentary on the text, brings familiar passages alive. These sections of John's sermons have been captured in a form that can be read by the teacher. Or, they can become a source of ideas as you tell the story in a narrative form that fits your style of communication.

New Testament Connection

There are many places where the Old Testament and New Testament intersect. Because most Christ-followers are more familiar with the New Testament, we have tried to make note of natural connection points between these two parts of the Bible. Sometimes the connection is linguistic, at other times it is thematic, and there are also times when a specific Old Testament passage is used in the New Testament. You will find helpful insights on how the Old Testament passage you are studying relates to familiar portions of the New Testament.

On the Lighter Side

Humor can be one of the greatest tools in a sermon. Jesus used irony and humor in his communication, and we can learn to use it as we teach God's Word. In these portions of the teacher's guide you will find two specific kinds of humorous insights. First, we will make note of biblical passages or insights that have a humorous aspect to them. Second, we will give you ideas for stories or jokes that might hit a main theme in the message.

Pause for Prayer

Too often a teacher waits until the end of a message to pray with God's people about what is being taught and learned. Sometimes the best time to pause for prayer is right in the middle of a message. If a point has a strong life application or potential for conviction and transformation, you might want to pause right in the midst of the message and take a few moments for prayer. The Pause for Prayer sections give suggestions for when you might want to do this and how to move naturally into prayer at these times.

Pause for Reflection

We live in a hurried world. Often, we preach and teach with the clock in mind. In our busy world, we need to be reminded that teaching God's Word should always include time for personal reflection. We need to make space for the Holy Spirit to speak to our hearts and touch our lives. The Pause for Reflection portions of the teacher's guide give the teacher ideas for possible times to pause, right in the middle of the message, and to take a moment for silence. These moments can be used to listen to God, process the lessons that have been learned, and reflect on personal life application goals.

Quotable Quote

God has spoken powerfully through many of his people through history. We have collected some great quotes from Christians throughout the ages and included them in the studies.

Significant Scripture

Every sermon in the OTC teacher's guide is rooted in Scripture. At the beginning of each section of each message is a list of significant Scriptures for that portion of the sermon. Most of the Scriptures listed are included in the message notes, but some are not. Occasionally we will list a related passage because we believe it would be worth studying as you prepare your message. Most of the time there is exposition of the passages listed in the Significant Scripture part of the study, but some of the time these are simply passages we encourage you to use for reflection as you prepare your message.

Word Study

Often the background of a word in the Bible helps a passage come alive and make sense. Any time we feel a word needs explanation, we include a short background piece in a word study. Sometimes these word studies give linguistic background; at other times they simply give a broader meaning for a word that might go unnoticed if not highlighted.

SESSION 1

Elijah: Holding Steady in a Roller Coaster World

1 KINGS 15:25–19:18

The Heart of the MESSAGE

In this life, we will have moments of great joy and intense sorrow. We will experience times of deep faith when God feels close and we see his power. We will also walk through the valley—times of confusion and darkness when God seems distant and removed. No matter what we face in this roller coaster life, we can hold steady because God is always with us, even when our eyes can't see him and our hearts can't feel him.

The Heart of the MESSENGER

Elijah is an amazing example of holding steady in a roller coaster world. He had times of astounding victory in his life when he saw the power of God pour down from heaven. He also had times of deep fear, insecurity, and even depression! He rode the roller coaster of life and faith and held on with all his might.

As you prepare to bring this message, take time to reflect on where you are in your life. Maybe you are in a season of joy, peace, and confident faith. Maybe you are discouraged and feel as if you are holding on for dear life. Maybe you are in the depths of depression and sadness. Wherever you are, God wants to speak to your heart and teach you about holding steady in your faith through this amazing ride we call life. God used Elijah to accomplish his purposes when he felt weak and when he felt strong, and God can use you to communicate this life-changing message right where you are today.

Brief Message OUTLINE

1. Elijah: Setting the Context
2. Elijah: Experiencing God's Power and Victory
3. Elijah: Meeting God in the Depths of Despair
4. Elijah: A Fresh Beginning

1. Elijah: Setting the Context

SIGNIFICANT SCRIPTURE

1 Kings 15:25-16:28

NARRATIVE ON THE TEXT | From Bad to Worse!

There is no question that Jeroboam was an evil king. At his death, God clearly declared that Jeroboam had done evil in the sight of God. He was so evil that other kings in the future were compared to him as a measuring rod in regard to how displeasing they were to God.

After Jeroboam died, his son Nadab takes the throne. He is as evil as his father. He is hated so much that he is killed by a man named Baasha. In short order, Baasha murders every single surviving member of Jeroboam's family to solidify his power and protect his throne.

Baasha is also an evil king, who misleads the people of Israel and pushes them away from God. His son Elah follows him and reigns for two years; he also is corrupt and evil. He is hated so much that he is killed by a man named Zimri.

SIGNIFICANT SCRIPTURE

1 Kings 16:29-34

Zimri reigns for only seven days. He can see that his reign will never last so he burns down the palace while he is inside of it. When Zimri dies, there is a civil war in the northern kingdom between Tibni and Omri. These two men battle to see who has the goofier name. Actually, they fight for the throne, and Omri wins. The text says that he is the worst king up to this point in Israel's history. Just imagine the climate in Israel at this time. King after king ascends to the throne, and each one is worse than the one before. Israel is spiraling deeper and deeper into sin. When things seem like they just can't get any worse, we are surprised!

HISTORICAL CONTEXT | A Divided Kingdom

If we think there is unrest in the Middle East in our day, we need to take a close look at the political climate that existed during the ministry of Elijah. God's people had been split in two through an intense civil war, never again to be a united nation. The northern kingdom of Israel and the southern kingdom of Judah are blood relatives who are now enemies as two distinct political entities. The northern kingdom's first king is Jeroboam. He is afraid that if the people of Israel who live in the north go down to Jerusalem to worship, he will lose control and their hearts will turn back to Jerusalem and Rehoboam, the king of the southern kingdom.

To keep the people from traveling to Jerusalem to worship God, Jeroboam sets up idols in in the cities of Dan and Bethel. He says to the people, "It's too much for you to go down to Jerusalem. That's too inconvenient. So here are your gods." Jeroboam has two golden calves made and set up as formal idols for the people to worship. The kingdom has been divided politically and geographically, but now Jeroboam makes sure that religious division is absolutely clear. In doing this, he leads the people into idolatry.

NARRATIVE ON THE TEXT | Meet the King and Queen

When Omri dies, his son Ahab becomes king. As hard as it might be to believe, Ahab takes evil to new heights and the people of Israel to new depths of sin. The writer of Kings puts it this way:

> Ahab son of Omri did *more evil in the eyes of the LORD than any of those before him*. He not only *considered it trivial to commit the sins of Jeroboam* son of Nebat, but he also *married Jezebel* daughter of Ethbaal king of the Sidonians, and began to *serve Baal and worship him*. He set up an altar for Baal in the temple of Baal that he built in Samaria. Ahab also made an Asherah pole and *did more to provoke the LORD, the God of Israel, to anger than did all the kings of Israel before him*. (1 Kings 16:30–33)

CREATIVE VIDEO ELEMENT

(VHS or DVD)

What's Up with That?
"The Village Hall" (4:50 min.)
This feature, hosted by Jarrett Stevens, answers tough questions from the Old Testament in an entertaining way. It can be used with any session.

Ahab marries a pagan wife from Sidon named Jezebel. She becomes famous for her hatred of God and his prophets. Ahab puts her in charge of religion, and her express agenda is to destroy the worship of Yahweh in all the land of Israel and to replace the one true God with her god, Baal. Up to this time, the people in the northern kingdom were at least attempting to worship Yahweh, though they used the golden calves to engage that worship rather than going to the temple in Jerusalem. But Jezebel sets her heart on replacing Israel's God with her idol god, Baal. Among other things, she seeks to systematically kill all of God's prophets. This is unprecedented. Past kings, even when they hated the prophets, wouldn't dare touch them. Not Jezebel—she has them killed with no indication that this bothers her at all.

This background is very important because Elijah's ministry begins when Ahab and Jezebel are leading Israel. This is clearly not a popular time to go into the ministry in the northern kingdom. Elijah is called by God and steps into ministry in a time of unparalleled tension, apostasy, and danger. This roller coaster time demands a prophet who can hold on and follow God through the highs and lows of doing ministry in such a climate.

2. Elijah: Experiencing God's Power and Victory

INTERPRETIVE INSIGHT | A Man of Courage

SIGNIFICANT SCRIPTURE

1 Kings 17:1-6

In these opening verses of 1 Kings 17 we see Elijah square off with King Ahab. Elijah says, "As the LORD, the God of Israel, lives, whom I serve, there will be neither dew nor rain in the next few years except at my word." Elijah is announcing a drought that is going to come as a judgment on Ahab. It is important to note that God chooses a drought as the sign of his judgment because Baal was said to be the god of the weather. God will soon be defining for everyone exactly who is the true God!

Imagine the courage it takes for Elijah to speak these words. This is the king who is the culmination of evil from a whole line of kings that just got worse and worse. This is the king who marries a pagan woman and allows her to kill the prophets. In the face of this fearless and hateful king, Elijah speaks a word of coming judgment. In a place where water and rainfall mean life and death, these words cause inexpressible anger and rage in Ahab. But when God calls Elijah to speak, he speaks!

INTERPRETIVE INSIGHT | God Provides in Surprising Ways

SIGNIFICANT SCRIPTURE

1 Kings 17:7–24

Not only is this woman a poor widow, she is also from Sidon. This is Jezebel's hometown, which means the woman is most likely a pagan. But God sees and God cares for this pagan widow and for his prophet Elijah.

The story is powerful and dramatic because when Elijah meets this woman and asks if she will feed him, she informs him that her situation is so desperate that her plan for that day is to make one final meal for her and her son and then to die of starvation! Just think about it. She has two items to check off her "To Do" list for the day:

- Fix a meal
- Die

Yet Elijah gives her hope. He assures her that if she takes what she has left and prepares a meal for him, she will still have enough for her and her son. Beyond that, Elijah lets her know that God will provide miraculous resources for them every day until the drought is over. What Elijah promised comes to pass. Every time she uses the flour and oil, there is more in the containers.

Their hopeless situation is turned upside down by God's surprising provision. Who would have dreamed that a pagan widow on the edge of poverty and starvation will be the one to have enough faith to give her final meal to a traveling prophet? Who would have dreamed that each day the jars will remain full of oil and flour? But this is just like God—his provision is often a mystery, but always enough.

ON THE LIGHTER SIDE | The First Fast Food

God tells Elijah to head east and hide in the Kerith Ravine that is to the east of the Jordan. This makes sense because Ahab is ready to kill Elijah after the words he has spoken. But with no rain in the forecast, how will Elijah eat and drink out in the desert? God tells Elijah that ravens will fly in and drop off bread and meat twice a day. This is the original fast food!

INTERPRETIVE INSIGHT | "But First"

The key phrase in the story of Elijah and the widow is when Elijah says, "But first." God's question of this widow is, "Will you trust me now with what you have?" Here is a lesson about human nature: *If you won't trust God now with what you have, you won't trust him when you get more.*

In verse 15 we read an amazing statement, "She went away and did as Elijah had told her." Think about the drama of this episode. This is a widow who is desperate. She is going to die. She takes the flour and oil—all that she has left—and prepares a meal for a man she just has met. Most of us would be tempted to make Elijah a very, very, very small loaf of bread—maybe a cracker-size loaf.

She does not do this. Before she prepares a funeral meal for herself and her son, she makes a cake of bread for Elijah. She makes a whole meal for Elijah, and she has nothing left. If God doesn't act, she and her son will die, and die without a final meal. But then, she looks into her oil and flour jars, and they are full! She and her son have enough to eat that day, and the next, and the next. One day at a time God meets the need of somebody who has no idea that there really is a God who sees and cares. She follows the "but first" invitation and never regrets it! She gives to Elijah first and never lacks for food again.

Give all He asks;
Take all He gives.
THOMAS R. KELLY

LIFE APPLICATION | Reckless Generosity

We should all pause occasionally and ask if we are living with the kind of reckless generosity we see in the life of the widow in this story. Maybe we have a whole lot of oil and flour in our jar. Maybe we only have a little. Maybe we have a large flour jar, or maybe a very small one. No matter what we have, we can still learn to live with a generous spirit.

Take time to ask some questions that will help people reflect on their own patterns of giving and generosity:

- Are you being faithful with your tithe to God?
- Are you being responsive to the needs of the poor?

PAUSE FOR PRAYER

Praise for Surprising Provision

You may want to pause right here in the message and lift up a prayer of thanks to God for his wonderful and surprising provision. If your congregation has experienced God's provision in recent days, lift up praise. Maybe there has been a time in the recent or distant past where God has poured out resources needed in your church; give him praise!

HISTORICAL CONTEXT | Widows in the Old Testament Days

When the drought gets bad and the stream dries up, God sends Elijah to a widow to be fed. At first glance, this may not seem strange, but in those days widows were the poorest and most vulnerable members of society. Because of the place of women in general and widows in particular, these are usually very poor people who are often outcasts. Yet, God chooses to use a poor widow to provide for his prophet.

- Are you learning to take risks in giving that stretches your faith?
- Are you giving in a way that is becoming a natural part of how you live?
- Are you noticing God's generous provision in your life and responding by growing more generous toward others?

NEW TESTAMENT CONNECTION

From the Lips of Jesus

Jesus had a great deal to say about how we use the resources in our care. The lessons from Elijah's life are reinforced by these words of Jesus: "Give, and it will be given to you. A good measure, pressed down, shaken together and running over, will be poured into your lap. For with the measure you use, it will be measured to you" (Luke 6:38).

Dallas Willard says the law of the kingdom is the law of inversion, where the last are first, and the servants are the greatest. This is modeled in a striking way in the life of this widow. The weakest, most vulnerable person, an impoverished, pagan, Gentile widow becomes the one whose generosity keeps the prophet Elijah alive.

INTERPRETIVE INSIGHT | Miracles

Later in the story the woman's son dies. But, Elijah prays, God sees and cares, and her son is restored. This woman comes to believe in the true God.

As you read through the lives of Elijah and Elisha, you will quickly notice that many miracles take place. In the Old Testament the miracles are not evenly distributed. They tend to come in bursts.

- At the time of the *Exodus* and the conquest of the land, there are the ten plagues, the parting of the Red Sea, the manna and the quail given in the desert, water from a rock, the parting of the Jordan, the walls of Jericho falling down, and many other miracles. At this time there are many miracles.

CREATIVE MESSAGE IDEA | Clusters of Miracles

Use a flip chart or overhead to draw a graph like you see here. Show the high points and peaks where there are many miracles. Note three of the times when many miracles are clustered together. Also show the valleys, where there is not much miraculous activity.

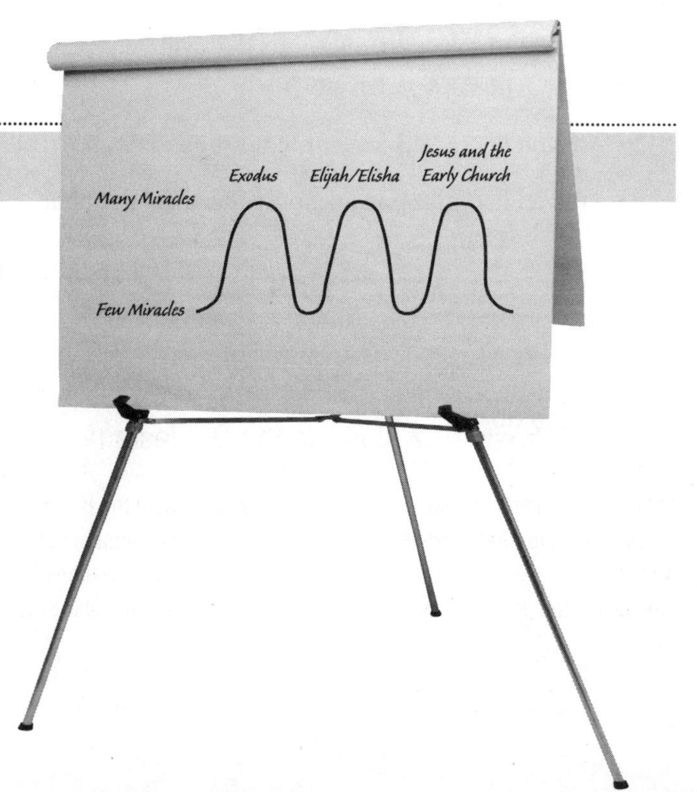

- In the era of *the judges and the kings* there are fewer miracles.
- When we come to the time of *Elijah and Elisha*, once again there is another amazing burst of miracles. Elijah prophesies that a drought is coming, and that is exactly what happens. Elijah is fed by ravens. There is the miracle of the widow's flour and oil and also her son being restored to life. Elijah predicts the coming of rain, and it starts to pour. He also foretells about the death of Ahab. Later, Elijah will be swept up into heaven by chariots of fire. Elisha's ministry, which follows Elijah's, is filled with as many miracles.
- The biblical record of miracles shows a drop-off during the *Exile* time of Israel's history.
- At the coming of *Jesus and Pentecost* in the early church, there was another huge burst of miracles—healings, deliverance from demons, and resurrections, to name just a few.

In the Old Testament miracles come at certain crucial moments in bursts of many astounding signs and wonders. This is important to note because sometimes people think that if they have strong faith, they will always be experiencing a string of spectacular, supernatural events. In the Scripture this is not the case. Miracles come in larger numbers at certain points, and we don't always know exactly why this is. Miracles come at key moments in the process of revelation. In the days of Elijah and Elisha God is seeking to build up and solidify his covenant people, and the miracles are part of that process.

WORD STUDY

Syncretism

Syncretism is the effort to embrace various religious systems at the same time. In the Old Testament, this practice occurs when God's people try to retain the practice of worshiping Yahweh, the God who has revealed himself to Abraham, Isaac, and Jacob, but they also try to adopt the religions of the nations around them. In many cases, it appears as if the people really believe they can hold onto worship of Yahweh with one hand and Baal with the other. Through time they have tried to adopt the religious practices and worship the idols of the Canaanites and other nations and still maintain their distinct worship of Yahweh.

LIFE APPLICATION | Syncretism Is Alive and Well

Many people still try to make room in their hearts for God and other religious systems. There are people who follow Jesus but also look to horoscopes or the stars to guide their lives. Others embrace the Christian faith with one hand and try to scoop up all they can from other world religions with the other.

HISTORICAL CONTEXT | A Critical Moment

It is crucial that we understand that in the era of Elijah and Elisha, worship of God is being threatened by the worship of Baal. The threat of idolatry, which has troubled Israel from the very beginning, has come to a crisis point. God is going to use Elijah to force Israel to choose between the false god Baal and the one true God of Israel. There is no room for holding on to this false pagan god and also embracing Yahweh, the true and living God.

The people don't yet know it, but they are racing full speed into a moment where they will decide their whole future as a nation. It is a moment of forced decision. Worship of idols is going to stop in Israel, or Israel will hit the end of the road. The whole issue of syncretism and God's people will be dealt with on Mount Carmel. This is a crucial moment in Israel's history.

PAUSE FOR REFLECTION

Has Syncretism Crept In?

You may want to pause for a brief time of reflection. Invite people to search their hearts and identify where idols have been set up or false gods are being worshiped. You may want to have someone play a few moments of quiet music during this time or simply leave things silent. Allow time for the Holy Spirit to search and identify places where syncretism has settled into the lives of God's people.

This is important because of the message that follows. In Elijah's confrontation with the prophets of Baal and his call to the people of Israel to make a choice whom they will follow, we all learn that God will not allow us to have our heart's devotion divided.

SIGNIFICANT SCRIPTURE

1 Kings 18

There are many expressions of syncretism in our world today, and God opposes them all. He is clear that our arms are not big enough to hold onto him and other false gods. If we are trying to keep a place in our heart for other "gods," we are living a syncretistic life and God has strong feelings about this that will be revealed as we continue looking at the life of Elijah. For now, we need to invite the Holy Spirit to search our hearts and see if we are seeking to embrace the one true God and some false god or idol.

NARRATIVE ON THE TEXT | You Troublemaker!

Elijah is commanded by God, after several years of drought, to go to Ahab. At this time, Ahab and his wife, particularly Jezebel, are systematically killing the prophets devoted to the God of Israel. God tells Elijah, "Go confront Ahab." When Ahab meets Elijah, he says to him, "Is that you, you troubler of Israel?" Ahab treats Elijah as if he is the one causing problems in Israel.

Elijah does not stand for this, and he turns the tables. In the face of the evil and murderous King Ahab, Elijah replied, "I have not made trouble for Israel . . . but you and your father's family have. You have abandoned the LORD's commands and have followed the Baals." Ahab points a finger at Elijah, and Elijah points right back at him.

NARRATIVE ON THE TEXT | The Battle Lines Are Drawn

Elijah tells Ahab what to do. He has him gather the people from all over Israel to meet on Mount Carmel so that they can settle this issue of religious syncretism once and for all. Elijah tells the king to bring all of the false prophets that Jezebel has set up in places of authority all over the land. This includes 450 prophets of Baal and 400 prophets of Asherah. All of these 850 are sponsored and supported by Jezebel. And Ahab does exactly as Elijah commands.

We must picture this scene on Mount Carmel. People from all over Israel have gathered. The 850 false prophets are there, and Elijah shows up. The whole country is gathered for this moment. On one side stand all the false prophets, the king, and all the power of his government and his army. On Ahab's side is the absolute license for the people to do whatever they feel like. There are no Ten Commandments there. There is no law about caring for orphans, widows, and aliens. There's no call for devotion to love God and neighbor. It's just idolatry that promises sexual pleasure as part of the cult worship and material abundance for all who bow down to Baal.

On the other side stands one man, one solitary prophet who emerges from years of hiding to confront a king and a country. But with that one man is God—Israel's God—the God who made them a people. The God of Abraham, Isaac,

Jacob, and Joseph is with Elijah. Standing with Elijah is the God who delivers meals by ravens and who fills the oil and flour jars of widows. To the naked eye, it seems as if Elijah is outnumbered 850 to 1. To the spiritual eye, Elijah is far from alone!

Standing in the middle are the people of Israel. They are at their critical deciding point. They have tried holding on to Yahweh and Baal. They have been living syncretistic lives, but now a line is being drawn.

INTERPRETIVE INSIGHT | The True Source of Authority

There is something striking in this story. Elijah is a runaway, fugitive preacher whom Jezebel is trying to kill. Ahab is the king of Israel who sits on the throne and has all authority in the nation of Israel. But notice who is giving the orders in this story: Elijah is! He has no office, no crown, no throne, but he says, "Do this," and the king does it. Where does he get such authority? This is the authority of one human being who is utterly yielded to God. It's a remarkable thing.

Ahab wears the crown. But Ahab is a man without a single, serious conviction. It's a miserable way to live. Ahab seems to become passive in the face of any strong character or conviction—whether it's Jezebel and evil, or Elijah and God. In this confrontation we see that Ahab has the official authority of the throne but no personal authority. Elijah has no human political authority, but God's presence in his life gives a greater strength and authority than Ahab will ever know.

INTERPRETIVE INSIGHT | Limping Along

In an act of immense courage, Elijah challenges a whole nation. He cries out the question that has been burning in the heart of God: "How long will you waver between two opinions? If the LORD is God, follow him; but if Baal is God, follow him."

Here is why Elijah is saying the people are wavering between two opinions: They don't think they have rejected Yahweh. They still pray to him if nothing else works. They just think they have added Baal to their religious portfolio. They have decided they will worship both. The word translated "waver" here literally means "to hobble" or "to limp."

The Hebrews would often use "walking" as a metaphor for life. Elijah is saying, "You are just limping through life. You have chosen a miserable way to live. You are being torn between two gods, and one of them is false." This image of limping speaks as loudly today as it did in the days of Elijah. When people try to follow the one true God and still embrace false gods, they will never walk securely, and they will certainly never run; they will limp along!

LIFE APPLICATION | Where Is Baal Today?

At this point it would be easy to dismiss this issue of syncretism and limping along as something that ended way back when people stopped bowing down to stone idols and when making sacrifices to the storm god ceased. But Baal is still alive and well. Anything we let take the place of God in our lives is idolatry. Often the things we try to embrace while we still hold on to God can become idolatrous and can cause us to limp along.

Take time to identify some of the ways that idolatry is still alive and well in the lives of Christ-followers today. Invite people to examine their hearts, with the help of the Holy Spirit, so that this will become a day when a line is drawn and each follower of Jesus declares that they will follow the one true God alone!

A Baal is *anything* that can tempt us away from full devotion to God. In other words, a Baal can be:

- a *relationship* that dishonors God
- a *lifestyle* that keeps you from being generous to the poor
- a *habit* or an *addiction* that you know God wants you to give up
- a *grudge* against someone who has really hurt you
- a struggle with *pride* and the power it has over you—perhaps the stubborn will to say, "I want to be in control of my own life. I want to call the shots."
- *anything that is diverting your devotion* from God

Maybe you've been telling yourself that you can hang on to your little Baal and hang on to God too. What God wants us to understand is that we can't. It is impossible! The process of trying to hold on to God and to Baal will make our lives miserable.

INTERPRETIVE INSIGHT | The People Say Nothing

When Elijah calls the people to a point of decision, we can almost feel the tension. They have grown used to embracing Yahweh and Baal. They like the freedom of options. They have become comfortable with the cultic prostitution and the open-minded posture of accepting every religious option on their spiritual horizons. Now they are being called to decide, to make a choice, to stand on one side of the line or the other.

This is an extraordinary moment. Hear the words again: "How long will you waver between two opinions? If the LORD is God, follow him; but if Baal is God, follow him" (1 Kings 18:21).

NEW TESTAMENT CONNECTION

You Can't Serve Two Masters

Elijah is expressing a fundamental spiritual truth. The human heart is only capable of giving its ultimate allegiance and devotion to one master. God has hard-wired us in such a way that we can't serve God and Baal and still remain healthy and thriving people. Jesus said it this way: "No one can serve two masters. Either he will hate the one and love the other, or he will be devoted to the one and despise the other. You cannot serve both God and Money" (Matthew 6:24).

Jesus is emphatic that his followers cannot love materials things with their whole hearts and still have room to love him with full devotion. They have to choose. This is the same message on the heart of God as he speaks through Elijah to the people. "No man can serve two masters," Elijah says. "If it's going to be Baal, at least be honest about it. Don't add hypocrisy to disobedience. Just be truthful. But if it's going to be God, then get right with God. Fall on your knees, confess, repent, and follow him. But one way or another, you must choose. It's decision time!"

What follows is staggering. We read the words: "But the people said nothing." No one knows how long this silence lasts, but it must have been deafening to Elijah and heartbreaking to God.

Can you imagine that moment? Some of the people are sullen. Some of them are defiant. Some are confused. Some are thinking, "Why should I have to choose? This life is working for me. Baal lets me do whatever I want. I can call on Yahweh anytime I really feel the need. Why should I change? I can follow my own agenda." No one says a word.

How sad that silence must have been for God. After all the centuries of his care and love for this people, nobody stands up for him. Nobody says a word. It's just dead silence. After parting seas, raining down manna, leading with a pillar of fire, breaking down walls, working mighty miracles for his people, they all stand in silence.

ILLUSTRATION | The Pain of Silence

Imagine a man and woman who have been dating for years. They have taken all the normal steps toward a growing and maturing relationship. They began as friends, and every indication is that they have fallen in love and are progressing forward. The man is certain she is the one. He is head over heals, punch-drunk, crazy in love with her. He shops and buys a beautiful diamond ring. He takes her to their favorite restaurant. He waits for the perfect moment. He slips out of his chair and takes a knee next to her. As he opens the jewelry box to reveal the ring, he says, "I love you, I want you to be my wife, will you marry me?"

Now imagine that she sits there in silence. She says nothing. For ten seconds, twenty, thirty, and a full sixty seconds, she says nothing. It feels like an eternity! Sometimes silence can be the loudest message of all.

NARRATIVE ON THE TEXT | 850 Voices Lifted with No Answer

Elijah and the prophets of Baal each build an altar, sacrifice a bull, and place it on a pile of wood on the altar. At this point in the sacrificial process, the normal next step is to set the wood on fire and let the flames consume the sacrifice. But, the

HISTORICAL CONTEXT | The "Nature God"

Baal was said to be the god of nature. He is pictured in ancient etchings with lightning bolts in his hand. The ancient writings say that Baal rode the thunderstorm as his chariot. In other words, a little fire from heaven should have been a piece of cake for Baal. If he really did exist, sending fire from heaven would have been in his job description! Since Baal was known as the "Nature God," the people would have seen this challenge as an easy task for him.

agreement is that neither will be allowed to set the wood on fire. This will be the job of their respective deity. Elijah will pray to Yahweh and ask him to reveal his presence and might through sending fire from heaven and igniting the wood. The 850 prophets will do the same as they call out to Baal to manifest his might through heavenly fire. Once the rules of engagement are established, all the people say, "What you say is good." They all agree that the one who answers with fire from heaven will be declared the true God!

The prophets of Baal call on him from morning until noon, but he does not respond. They cry out, "O Baal, answer us!" but there is silence. No one answers. They dance around the altar and unite their 850 voices, but the heavens remain silent.

NARRATIVE ON THE TEXT | They Just Don't Get It!

We learn quickly that the prophets of Baal don't have much of a sense of humor, or maybe they just don't catch the tone of subtle sarcasm. They take Elijah seriously and decide, "Yeah, Elijah is right. We've got to work harder to try to get Baal's attention." They shout louder and slash themselves with swords and spears. They try to get Baal's attention by making themselves bleed. What a sad testimony to the utter emptiness of this false religious system.

Midday passes, and they are exhausted and bleeding! Yet, they continue their frantic prophesying until the time for the evening sacrifice. With all their yelling and signs of religious devotion, there is no response. No one answers. No one pays attention.

ON THE LIGHTER SIDE | Where Is Your God?

At this point in the drama Elijah wants to make sure that everybody understands the absolute absurdity of putting trust in Baal—a nonexistent god. In 1 Kings 18:27 Elijah engages in a little prophetic trash talk. Listen to Elijah's words:

> "Shout louder!" he said. "Surely he is a god! Perhaps he is deep in thought, or busy, or traveling. Maybe he is sleeping and must be awakened." (1 Kings 18:27)

This passage is a little hard to translate, but clearly Elijah is intending to use mockery, humor, and sarcasm to show how ridiculous it is to pray to a god who isn't there. Elijah lays it on quite thick. *The Living Bible* (with good indication from the sense of the Hebrew in this passage) translates the passage like this:

> "You'll have to shout louder than that to catch the attention of your god. Maybe he's talking to someone or out sitting on the toilet."

Elijah is going full throttle. He's trying anything to show the people how crazy this is. You can almost hear Elijah taunt, "Maybe your god suffers from irregularity."

INTERPRETIVE INSIGHT | A Decisive Turning Point

This is a magnificently written account. The prophets of Baal go on for hours until it is the official time for the evening sacrifice that would normally be made to the God of Israel. Elijah finally just puts an end to the craziness. He calls the people over to him and carefully prepares the altar. He pours water over the sacrifice three times to make it even harder for the wood to ignite and to make sure everyone knows that only God could light this fire. Then he prays. But his prayer is an absolute contrast to the wild excesses of the behavior of the prophets of Baal.

He simply prays:

> "O LORD, God of Abraham, Isaac and Israel, let it be known today that you are God in Israel and that I am your servant and have done all these things at your command. Answer me, O LORD, answer me, so these people will know that you, O LORD, are God, and that you are turning their hearts back again." (1 Kings 18:36–37)

God sees and cares, and fire comes down from heaven and consumes the offering, the wood, the water, the soil, and the stones! God wins the battle, hands down!

This is a decisive turning point in the history of Israel. All the people who stand in muted silence up to this point now begin to cry out, "The LORD—he is God! The LORD—he is God!" The prophets of Baal are defeated and the nation returns to Yahweh.

LIFE APPLICATION | How Do We Pray?

It is helpful to pause for a moment and observe the vivid contrast between the way the prophets of Baal prayed and the way Elijah prayed. The 850 false prophets yelled, screamed, acted out, and put on a show. Elijah simply spoke and watched God manifest his power.

This is important to note because sometimes Christians pray more like the prophets of Baal than like Elijah. They pray as if they think that they have to get God's attention by doing something dramatic. Some followers of Christ believe they must pray loud enough, long enough, with the right formula, with enough boldness, or with some kind of radical and special behavior if God is going to hear. This is simply not true. Elijah talks to God calmly and expects God to take care of the results.

3. Elijah: Meeting God in the Depths of Despair

SIGNIFICANT SCRIPTURE

1 Kings 19:1-9

INTERPRETIVE INSIGHT | From the Mountain to the Valley

How many people in the history of the human race have ever experienced manifestations of the power of God as Elijah did? He saw God work in ways most of us could never even dream possible. Yet, right after seeing God pour fire from heaven and defeat the prophets of Baal, things take a dramatic turn for Elijah.

When Jezebel hears of Elijah's triumph over her prophets, she vows to see him dead. Elijah, who defied a king, defeated 850 prophets, and confronted an entire nation single-handedly, runs in fear at the threat of one queen. This turnabout is so sudden and so dramatic that some Old Testament scholars are convinced that this part of the story is out of place. However, there is nothing in the text, or in life, that supports this idea.

Elijah experiences what many followers of Christ have gone through. After a mountaintop experience of intense intimacy with God and awareness of God's presence, Elijah hits a low point in his spiritual life. He seems to enter a time of fear and even depression. Elijah goes from the mountain to the valley in a very short time.

ON THE LIGHTER SIDE | Time for a Run

Now Elijah gives Ahab another command. He says, "Go, eat and drink, for there is the sound of a heavy rain." Remember, there hasn't been rain for years and there's not a cloud in the sky. But Elijah says, "It's going to rain." Next Elijah sends his servant to give the king instructions. This time Elijah does not even bother going to the king, but he has a servant give a secondhand command to the ruler of Israel. Ahab is told to ride in his chariot to the palace in Jezreel.

Elijah decides he's going to jog back to Jezreel. In 1 Kings 18:46 we read, "And the power of the LORD came upon Elijah and, tucking his cloak into his belt, he ran ahead of Ahab all the way to Jezreel."

Here's the kicker: The run from Mount Carmel to Jezreel is about sixteen miles. Can you imagine trying to outrun a chariot in a sixteen-mile race?

Now, you have to imagine Ahab sitting in his chariot. All he can think of is Elijah. Elijah who called for a drought that could ruin him; Elijah who eluded him for years; Elijah who goes around giving him orders; Elijah who had single-handedly challenged all the prophets of Baal and destroyed them. Certainly Ahab is also thinking about how he will tell Jezebel that all of her 850 prophets are now dead and her whole religious takeover of Israel has been crushed by one man—Elijah.

You can almost see Ahab in his chariot riding along and thinking, "At least in my chariot I get a break from Elijah. I'll have a few hours when I get to Jezreel, before Elijah arrives, to get a break from this guy!" Then Ahab looks and sees something staggering. There is Elijah, running faster than his horse-drawn chariot. Elijah waves at him as he's running by: "See you at the palace."

Elijah has outfoxed Ahab's soldiers and outprayed Ahab's prophets, and now he's outrunning Ahab's horses!

NARRATIVE ON LIFE | We All Visit the Valley

Nobody stays on top of the mountain forever—nobody. We will all have spiritual peaks and valleys as long as we live. Sometimes, after an unbelievable, adrenaline-filled, record-setting run of achievement and spiritual victory, we can find ourselves in the most vulnerable times of doubt, fear, or depression. The question is not, "Will I ever visit the valley?" The real issue is, "How will I respond when I visit the valley?"

NARRATIVE ON THE TEXT | Praying from the Depths

Elijah is about to snap. The same Elijah who prayed and fire came down from heaven to consume a sacrifice, who prayed for rain and a drought ended, who received the strength to outrun a chariot, prays for one more thing: "Let me die." How much lower can a person go!

But the good news is that God loves a person so much that sometimes he answers that prayer in the way it is asked. Elijah is so down that he does not know how he can press on, yet God still has a plan for Elijah. God hears Elijah's honest and passionate prayer. He is down, he is discouraged, and he feels he can't go on, so he tells God just how he feels. Elijah prays from the depths, God hears from the heights, and God prepares to lift Elijah out of the pit.

Extraordinary afflictions are not always the punishment of extraordinary sins, but sometimes the trial of extraordinary graces. Sanctified afflictions are spiritual promotions.
MATTHEW HENRY

CREATIVE MESSAGE IDEA | Map Time

Elijah goes on quite a journey. You may want to use the Power Point slide provided in the kit to show where God leads him. Elijah goes from Jezreel to Beersheba (in the southern kingdom), to the Negev, and into the desert, which is outside the boundaries of Israel.

ON THE LIGHTER SIDE | Snack Time

It is wonderful to see what happens after Elijah's despairing prayer. He falls asleep, and while he gets some much needed rest, God sends an angel to help him. The angel brings a cake and some water. When Elijah wakes up, the angel has him eat, drink, and then take another nap!

God treats Elijah the way you treat a cranky two-year-old. "Here are some Twinkies and some juice. Have a snack and take a nap." Elijah does as he is told, and when he wakes up, he feels a lot better—so much better that he is ready to travel for forty days and nights.

4. Elijah: A Fresh Beginning

SIGNIFICANT SCRIPTURE

1 Kings 19:10–18

INTERPRETIVE INSIGHT | A Time of Depression

When Elijah reaches the Negev, at least geographically, he has left the people of Israel. He is far from God's people. In a sense, he has left his post. That's why God says, "What are you doing here?" Elijah is running away from what God has for him to do. He has classic signs of depression: suicidal thoughts, loss of appetite, and a distorted perspective on reality.

And you can bet that inside of his mind a little voice is saying things like, "You call yourself a prophet? You have more doubt and fear than the people you preach to. You ran out on God after all he did for you. You left the people just when they started turning from Baal and needed you most. There's no way God could ever use somebody like you."

Elijah must have felt like we all do on some days. He must have had a sense that he was not real useful for God's purposes and that his future was pretty bleak.

NARRATIVE ON THE TEXT | A Whole New Start

But God sees and God cares. God does an amazing thing. Elijah pours out his heart, and God begins a process of giving him a whole new beginning. God calls him out of a cave and into the light. On the mountain Elijah stands and waits for the Lord to pass by. First, there is a powerful wind, then an earthquake, and finally a fire. But God is not in these things. Finally, there is a gentle whisper and God is there, with Elijah, showing him that he still sees and cares.

At this time, God lets Elijah know that he can have a whole new start. He reminds him that he is not alone and that there are many who still follow Yahweh. And, best of all, God begins to reveal his plan to bring a new friend into Elijah's life, a man named Elisha, who will follow in his steps as a prophet. God is not even close to being done with working in Elijah's life.

CREATIVE MESSAGE IDEA | Communion

At the table of Jesus we find one of the best reminders that God offers a new beginning to all who ask. You might want to consider having communion together at the end of this message. In Exodus, and scattered throughout the whole rest of the Pentateuch, we find every one of these features. God is all about covenant.

What we have to keep in the forefront of our minds is that the laws were never intended to be a list of rules that somebody had to keep to earn salvation. These laws were given after God had redeemed his people from Egypt and called them his beloved children. They were intended to describe *what a covenant relationship with God was supposed to look like.* What would it look like to be a kingdom of priests and a holy nation?

LIFE APPLICATION | The God of New Beginnings

Sometimes when people are hurting, what they need most of all is a sense of purpose. God often brings renewal by giving new meaning and life direction. That is the gift God gives to Elijah. Elijah goes back down the mountain and begins a whole new chapter in his adventure with God.

This may be the gift God wants to give to many people who hear this message. There may be people who feel discouraged, depressed, and even useless to God. But every follower of Christ can be confident that honest expression in prayer, even in the hardest times, can lead to a new beginning and even fresh life direction.

The lament is an appeal to God's compassion to intervene and change a desperate situation . . . they raise a cry out of the depths in the confidence that God has the power to lift a person out of the "miry bog" and set one's feet upon a rock. Hence the laments are really expressions of praise—praise offered in a minor key in the confidence that Yahweh is faithful and in anticipation of a new lease on life.

BERNHARD W. ANDERSON

Elisha: Receiving a Spiritual Legacy

SESSION
2

1 KINGS 19:15–21; 2 KINGS 2:1–15; 4:1–7; 6:8–23

The Heart of the **MESSAGE**

It has often been said that the Christian faith is always one generation away from extinction. If we don't pass the flame of faith to the next generation, it will not continue. Of course God is always active in accomplishing his purposes, but he invites us to be part of his plan in the world.

In this session we will look at how God calls Elijah to pass on the flame of faith to the next generation. His flame is given to Elisha, and he, in turn, continues to pass it on. In a similar way, followers of Christ today are invited into the joy-filled experience of investing their lives and faith in another generation of believers. It may be a class of children taught during a Sunday school hour. It could be high school students in a youth group that receive the flame. For many it will be their sons and daughters and grandchildren. There are also those who will become spiritual sons and daughters, much like Elisha becomes a spiritual son to Elijah. Whoever it is, God calls us to be ready to invest our lives in passing the torch of faith to the next generation and so leave a spiritual legacy.

Brief Message **OUTLINE**

1. A Call to Bear the Torch
2. Elijah Passes the Torch to Elisha
3. Elisha Carries the Flame

The Heart of the **MESSENGER**

Take time to reflect in two different directions as you prepare to bring this message. First, think about those who have passed on the flame of faith to you over the years. Thank God for their lives and faithfulness. Next, think about those whom God has placed in your life and to whom you are called to pass the torch. Pray for boldness, consistency, and wisdom as you continue to follow God's leading in passing on a spiritual legacy to others.

1. A Call to Bear the Torch

ILLUSTRATION | Passing the Torch

In ancient Greece when it was time for the Olympic Games, athletes from around the country would be handed a torch with a special flame. Every one of them would run their leg of the race and then hand off their torch to the next runner. Eventually the torch would make it to an altar in Olympia and remain there. Other flames came and went but this one was never to be extinguished.

This was a sacred matter to the Greek people. The flame symbolized the light of spirit and knowledge and life that gets passed down from one generation to another. These people considered themselves keepers of the flame. They were passers of the torch.

LIFE APPLICATION | Looking Back and Looking Forward

Every follower of Christ is where he or she is because somebody passed on the torch of faith. Maybe it was parents, grandparents, a teacher, a Sunday school teacher, a schoolteacher, a pastor, or someone else, but somebody nurtured our faith. Someone prayed, invested, loved, and let the flame burn bright in his or her life. It is terribly important that we all understand that in every generation,

CREATIVE MESSAGE IDEA | Lighting the Torch

If you want to use a visual reminder of what's at stake in this call to pass on a spiritual legacy, you might look into lighting a torch that you will keep burning throughout the entire message. If you have issues of fire code, be sure to get the right permissions and have a fire extinguisher handy. You may even want to invite someone from the local fire department to be on hand and ensure everything stays safe and sane!

HISTORICAL CONTEXT | The Flame from the Beginning

God lit the flame and passed it on from the beginning. It really started with Adam and Eve. Later, Abraham passed the torch to Isaac, and he handed it to Jacob, who in turn passed the torch to Joseph. In the Bible we learn that passing the flame does not just happen between parents and children. Moses passed the torch on to Joshua. Eli did the same with young Samuel. Jesus passed the torch to his apostles. The apostle Paul, as an old man, celebrated as he saw the flame of faith ignite in Timothy's life.

From the beginning, it was God's plan that his followers be torchbearers. If we fail to rise up to this calling, each new generation is at risk! The question God is asking is clear: "Will somebody guard the flame? Will we continue the legacy and pass on the torch to the next generation?"

from Abraham's to ours, somebody passed the torch to somebody else and then to somebody else. Not a single generation was skipped. That's why we are where we are today.

Take a moment to reflect on these questions:

- Whom did God use to pass on the flame of faith to me?
- Who has prayed for me, loved me, and let their light shine for me?
- Who has been a torchbearer in my life?
- How can I thank or bless those who have passed on the torch in my life?

Next, take a moment to reflect on these questions:

- Do I have people in my life to whom I am passing the torch?
- In whom am I investing myself?
- Am I keeping the flame bright in my life so that the torch gets passed on to others?
- Who are specific people God has placed in my life so that I can pass the flame to them?
- What are some of the steps I can take to be a torchbearer more intentionally in the lives of others?

CREATIVE MESSAGE IDEA | Putting It on Paper

Invite everyone to write down the names of two kinds of people in their lives. First, have those gathered write down the names of those who have passed on the torch of faith to them. Second, have them write down at least one or two names of people to whom they feel God wants them to pass the flame in the coming weeks and months. It would be helpful if you had a card that you gave each person as they entered the worship service or class where this message will be communicated. There is an example of a simple card you can create printed below. After each person has written down a few names, encourage them to put this card somewhere where they will see it on a regular basis.

Receiving and Giving a Spiritual Legacy

People who have passed on the torch of faith to me:	People to whom God wants me to pass the flame:
•	•
•	•

2. Elijah Passes the Torch to Elisha

NARRATIVE ON THE TEXT

When Elijah was on the mountain, God spoke to him. Elijah was in despair and was pouring his heart out to God. In the middle of this low point in his life, God lets him know that he is not done passing on his flame. There is a man named Elisha who needs the leadership Elijah has to offer. God lets Elijah know that he will be grooming Elisha to be the new prophet in Israel.

NARRATIVE ON LIFE You Won't Always Be Israel's Prophet!

SIGNIFICANT SCRIPTURE
1 Kings 19:15-16

In 1 Kings 19:15–16 God is telling Elijah that he will be anointing two kings. Then God just slips this in: "And, by the way, you will also be anointing your replacement." How do you think Elijah feels when he hears those words? It takes a certain kind of humility to do what Elijah is called to do.

Up to this point, Elijah has been the key prophet for God in Israel. When you are a prophet, you tend to get a certain amount of attention, and your role carries a certain measure of power. Elijah is informed that he will be giving up his place as the number one prophet in the land. Elijah is going to have to acknowledge that a younger man will take over for him. He must face the reality that a new prophet will replace him and that Elisha may even go further than Elijah did.

NARRATIVE ON THE TEXT

SIGNIFICANT SCRIPTURE
1 Kings 19:19-21

Elijah does exactly what God asks. He is ready to pass the flame, and Elisha is the one God has chosen. Elijah comes down the mountain and sees Elisha plowing in the field. All the people there know who Elijah is, and here is Elisha out doing his work and he sees Elijah, Israel's prophet, coming right toward him. When he reaches Elisha, Elijah takes off his cloak and drapes it around Elisha's shoulders.

CREATIVE MESSAGE IDEA Torch-bearing Testimonies

You may want to consider having one or two pairs of people share a brief testimony about how they have passed and received the torch of faith. This can be a parent and child, a youth and an adult, or any pair of people who have a story to tell about how one of them has invested in the life of the other and passed on the flame. Allow one to tell the story from the perspective of passing on a spiritual legacy and the other to tell about what it means to them to have received a spiritual legacy. This can be done live or on video.

There is no report that he says a word. He simply places the cloak over his shoulders, turns, and walks away.

In the King James Version, this cloak is called a "mantle." Today, when we talk about a mantle of responsibility or a mantle of leadership getting passed on, it comes from this story. In a visible way, Elijah is saying to Elisha, "I am inviting you to follow me and learn from me. I want to walk with you and teach you. I want to have you watch what I do and then see how God can also work in and through your life." In a real sense, Elijah is saying, "I want to pass the flame to you. I want to give you the spiritual legacy God has given to me. I want your flame to burn brighter and brighter, and one day you will lead as the prophet in Israel without me even being at your side."

ILLUSTRATION | The Role of Mentors

In our world today there is often talk of mentors. These are people who pass on a legacy in the business world, athletics, or some other area of life. Many people see the value of going through an internship or mentoring relationship before they step out on their own. If this is important in the world of business or athletics, how much more important when it comes to the eternal issues of life.

NARRATIVE ON LIFE | Making Sacrifices

What Elijah is asking Elisha to do involves enormous sacrifice. The Bible says nothing about Elijah's background. He may very well have been from a poor family. He may not have had too many career options. But Elisha is another story. Elisha's got it made. He will inherit a way of life that will keep him comfortable for the rest of his days.

But God has called Elijah to ask Elisha to walk away from his secure and wealthy lifestyle and follow him on a path that may very well lead to poverty, rejection, and the opposition of stubborn kings who want him dead. From the beginning, Elisha must have realized that following God's plan for his life would mean making significant sacrifices.

PAUSE FOR PRAYER

Praise and Power

Take time to pray for God to move followers of Christ in two different directions. First, ask for a sense of praise and thankfulness to overflow for those who have passed on the torch of faith to us. Celebrate how God has used family members, friends, Sunday school teachers, youth leaders, pastors, and others to pass on the flame. Second, ask for the power of the Holy Spirit to fill each Christ-follower with the strength and boldness they need to be a bearer of the torch and a keeper of the flame. Ask God to help us pass the flame to a new generation.

Also, pray for those attending who are still spiritual seekers. Give thanks to God that they have people in their life who love them enough to want to pass on the flame of faith. Pray for them to find joy as they continue their journey. Pray that if they come to a place when they receive Christ as their personal forgiver and leader, they will one day become passers of the torch of faith.

HISTORICAL CONTEXT | A Rich Kid

When Elijah comes to Elisha and invites him to follow in the steps of the prophet, it will involve great commitment and sacrifice on the part of Elisha. Take note of the number of oxen Elisha is plowing with. In that day, most families were poor enough that they might own a few chickens. For a family to own one ox was quite rare and a sign of wealth. They'd be fairly well off. To have twelve teams of oxen (twenty-four) was almost unheard of. This is an indication that Elisha's family are people of immense wealth. In contemporary terms, they had a huge house in the most wealthy neighborhood in town and a condo in Maui. Elisha is a rich kid, no question about it!

At the same time, Elijah knows, from personal experience, that he is calling Elisha to give up more than he could dream, in terms of earthly things. It would have been so easy for Elijah to say, "God, you made a mistake. Elisha is not going to walk away from a great future like that to follow a prophet like me. He's got too many attractive options. You've got the wrong guy. He would never do something like this. I'm not even going to ask."

NEW TESTAMENT CONNECTION

The Example of Jesus

Jesus knew the absolute importance of passing on a spiritual legacy. He had many groups of people who followed him and learned from his example. There was a group of seventy-two people who had access to Jesus and who learned from him (Luke 10). He also had a group of twelve (Matthew 10:1-2), and finally, there were Peter, James, and John (Matthew 17:1). These last three received close instruction and were invited to learn from Jesus at the most critical moments of his life and ministry. Jesus' example of passing on a spiritual legacy and the flame of faith should inspire each of us to do the same.

LIFE APPLICATION

Never Say "No" for Someone Else

It would have been so easy for Elijah to walk right past Elisha and look for someone who seemed more likely to say yes. But, that is not what he does. Elijah makes the big ask. He places the mantle over Elisha's shoulders and invites him into a whole new life!

What happens next is a joy to see. Elisha takes the challenge, receives the invitation, and begins a whole new life. Because of Elijah's courage to ask and Elisha's willingness to follow, Israel is changed and the world is changed.

What a powerful reminder for each of us that it is never our place to say "no" for someone else. We must never assume that somebody doesn't want to get involved, learn, grow, and serve just because it might not make sense to us. Never assume that anybody has too many options that are more attractive to them than living and serving in the kingdom of God. God knows that so many people are one conversation away from being a keeper of the flame and a carrier of his message.

LIFE APPLICATION

The Important Place of Celebration

When Elisha volunteers and decides to follow Elijah, this is a significant event in his life. It needs to be acknowledged and even celebrated. So, they have a big

HISTORICAL CONTEXT

What They Said and What They Meant

When Elijah places his cloak over Elisha and extends the invitation to follow him, Elisha's response is, "Let me kiss my father and mother good-bye, then I'll come with you." This may seem a little ambiguous to us, but it would not have seemed strange back in the Old Testament days. In Middle Eastern culture it was extremely rude to say an outright "no" to somebody. That would be very impolite.

Thus, when Elisha gives this response, it could be just what it looks like on the surface, but it could also be his way of asking for more time to think about it. It could be a polite way of trying to say, "I'm not sure, or I am not ready to commit, but give me time."

Notice Elijah's response, "Go back to your parents," he says. "What have I done to you?" In other words, Elijah is saying is, "I'm not going to use any guilt. I'm not going to use any pressure. I want you to be free in this decision. It is your call."

party. What is recorded here is a brief account of something that would have taken a considerable amount of time to plan. It may well be that Elijah and Elisha plan the celebration together.

They decide the appropriate celebration will be a huge barbecue. The word "huge" might not really hit the mark. Look at it this way: Have you ever seen a side of beef? Can you imagine how many people you can feed with two oxen? Oxen are big animals. Elijah and Elisha put on an enormous feast to celebrate this step in Elisha's life. Friends and family affirm his decision.

We need to learn from this example in our homes, relationships, and churches. When people say yes to a volunteer place of ministry, it is a big deal! When somebody volunteers and says, "Yes, I will! I don't have to do it, I have other options, but I'm going to devote myself to the task God has placed before me," this deserves celebration.

It is important in the life of the church to make time to rejoice over those who are serving God as volunteers. We need to have a barbecue, throw a party, publicly bless and pray for people, and do all we can to celebrate those who follow God's example of being a volunteer.

Never insult anybody by asking them to do an easy job.
MAX DEPREE

When volunteers are asked how they happened to get involved in their particular activity, the most common answer is, "Somebody asked me." Conversely, when people are asked why they did not volunteer or donate, they say, "Nobody asked."
ROBERT PUTNAM

NARRATIVE ON LIFE | Leaving the Past Behind

Once Elisha has made the decision to become a volunteer and follow Elijah, he does something dramatic. If you read too quickly, you might miss it. As part of the big barbecue celebration party, Elisha uses his plowing equipment to set the fire and roast his oxen. In other words, his primary past occupation and source of wealth all go up in smoke. He is not leaving an easy door open to return to his past life. He knows God is calling and he is ready to follow, so he closes the door on his past through a dramatic gesture of burning his plowing equipment and serving his oxen up for a community feast.

CREATIVE MESSAGE IDEA | Guilt in the Church?

Have you ever heard of a church using guilt or pressure to try to get someone to volunteer to do something? There is a powerful little clip of Bill Hybels telling about how a pastor tried to manipulate members of his congregation into volunteering to be Sunday school teachers by talking about how little fourth grade kids end up on drugs if they don't have a good Sunday school class. This story can be found at the start of the Networking video in the kit published by Zondervan and Willow Creek.

WORD STUDY

Volunteer

Elijah shows tremendous respect and honor toward Elisha. If Elisha follows, it will be his choice, and he will never be able to say that Elijah has forced him. Elisha is really a volunteer. Our word "volunteer" comes from a Latin word, which means "will" or "choice." We sometimes think of a volunteer as somebody who is not getting paid. But at its core, volunteer means something much more. A volunteer is someone who freely embraces a task, even though he or she doesn't have to, even though he or she has other options. A volunteer willingly chooses to devote oneself to a task he or she doesn't have to do.

SIGNIFICANT SCRIPTURE

2 Kings 2:1-15

NARRATIVE ON LIFE

A Humble Spirit

Once the party is over, we read that Elisha "set out to follow Elijah and became his attendant." The idea of Elisha's following is not just geographical. It is a matter of submission. He's going to become a follower of Elijah. Specifically, he becomes his "attendant." We see the humility of Elisha from the very beginning. He gives up a privileged position as a wealthy heir—a man who's got it made—to become a learner, a student, a follower, a servant, of Elijah.

When we look for somebody to pass the torch on to, we need to look for somebody who has a coachable spirit and a humble heart. Elisha is so eager to learn that he becomes an attendant to Elijah. Part of what makes the relationship between Elijah and Elisha work is the humility on both sides. Elijah doesn't claim to be the only prophet. Elisha doesn't demand to be the star. They become passers of the torch together.

NARRATIVE ON THE TEXT

A Strange Journey

Elijah and Elisha begin their journey in *Gilgal*, which is close to the Jordan River. Elijah tells Elisha to stay there while he goes on to Bethel. But Elisha said, "As surely as the LORD lives and as you live, I will not leave you." This is a strong response from Elisha. He lets Elijah know, "Nothing doing. I'm going to stick with you." So Elijah moves on, and Elisha goes with him.

Next they go to *Bethel*, which is inland almost halfway to the Mediterranean Sea. Once they are in Bethel, they go through the same set of speeches. Elijah tells him to wait there, and Elisha is emphatic that he is not leaving Elijah's side.

They travel on to *Jericho*. In Jericho they echo the same conversation and move on. Finally, they end up at the *Jordan River*. This seems like a strange journey, and the recurring conversation between these two prophets can seem quite odd. But, the issue at hand seems to be a test to see if Elisha is fully committed to following Elijah, and ultimately, following God.

ON THE LIGHTER SIDE

A Teachable Spirit

A father was sitting in church with his three-year-old son. The message was being given and the boy was really paying attention. But, the little boy was also wiggling and it looked as if he might have to go to the bathroom. Finally the little boy expressed the problem to his dad. He said, "Dad, I gotta go potty, but I don't want to miss this point."

That is a teachable spirit! That is a little boy who will learn much, because his heart longs to learn, even beyond the capacity of his little bladder.

INTERPRETIVE INSIGHT

Unshakable Loyalty

We don't know exactly why Elijah keeps telling Elisha to stay behind. Maybe Elijah wants to face the end alone. Maybe he's afraid what he is going to experience will be too much for Elisha to handle. Maybe it is a test to see if Elisha proves to be a follower of unshakable loyalty. No matter what the reason, the result is clear to see. Elisha is so committed to following his leader that he proves a level of loyalty that is tenacious and unshakable. Like a bulldog with his teeth locked onto a steak, Elisha will not let go of his mentor and friend.

Not only is there no jealousy or rivalry between these men, there is deep affection and God-honoring friendship. When the torch is passed the right way, it can create extraordinary oneness and community.

NARRATIVE ON THE TEXT

A Wonderful Gift

Finally the two of them come to the Jordan River. They know their time together is short. Elijah takes off his mantle—the same one he spread over Elisha so long ago—wraps it up, and strikes the River Jordan. Just as the water separated a long time ago for Moses and for Joshua, now it separates for Elijah.

The two of them cross over together on dry ground. They leave the Promised Land, the ordinary world, for an extraordinary event. At this decisive moment Elijah does a wonderful thing. He is about to leave this world and Elisha's side. But he doesn't give a lot of advice, instructions, or commands. Elijah simply asks Elisha one last question.

Like all great questions, this one is a little bit of a test. It's a little like the question God asked Solomon, "What do you want if I could give you anything?" Specifically, Elijah asks Elisha, "What can I do for you before I am taken from you?" What a great question! This is a question that every torch-passer should learn to ask, "What can I do for you?"

LIFE APPLICATION

How Can I Help You Become All God Wants You to Be?

Before we look at Elisha's response, think of those to whom you are called to pass the torch. How often do you say, "What can I do for you?" How often do you ask them how God might use you to help them become more of what he wants? How can you begin asking the kind of questions that will help you learn how God can use you more effectively as a bearer of the torch and passer of the flame?

NARRATIVE ON THE TEXT

The Flame Is Passed

Elisha asks for exactly the right thing. Elijah lets him know that what he has asked for is difficult, but not impossible. When it comes to choosing his successor, in the final view, no mere human being can do that. Elijah can help, shape, and encourage, but ultimately Elisha's work is between him and God.

NEW TESTAMENT CONNECTION

The Volunteering Heart of God

A scholar named Brackley notices the fundamental heart of a volunteer is much like the heart of God. He says, "This is moving to us, because it flows out of the nature of a God who voluntarily gives himself to his people." In John 10:17–18 we read:

> The reason my Father loves me is that I lay down my life—only to take it up again. No one takes it from me, but I lay it down of my own accord. I have authority to lay it down and authority to take it up again. This command I received from my Father.

Jesus reveals the heart of a volunteer. His life declares this message: "I volunteered to leave heavenly glory, I volunteered to be born in a stable, I volunteered to suffer and die on a cross. I willingly chose this assignment. I didn't have to do it, but I gladly volunteered!"

The Father loves to see a volunteer stand up and say, "I will do it!" That's why the church has always been, and always will be, fundamentally a volunteer-based organization.

CREATIVE MESSAGE IDEA

Map Time

You may want to show the route Elijah and Elisha take as they walk together on their final journey. There are slides in the Power Point presentation that show where they travel.

But Elijah says, "If you see me when I'm taken from you, it will be yours." Tension is now introduced to the story. Not only is Elisha going to lose Elijah, he doesn't know if his own ministry is just beginning or about to end.

As they wait to see what God is going to do, they walk together. This is a beautiful picture of two friends walking along the Jordan side by side. We can only imagine what is going through their minds. They have traveled so many miles together. God has used them to do amazing things. They have forged a friendship. Soon, Elisha will be alone. What will his future look like?

Suddenly, out of nowhere, a chariot of fire and horses of fire appear, and Elijah and Elisha are separated from each other. Elijah is swept up into the arms of God, and Elisha is left behind. Elisha cries out, "My father! My father!" He sees the whole thing. His friend, mentor, and leader is gone so he tears his garments—a sign of grief and loss.

Elisha looks down on the ground and sees Elijah's cloak. It's his reminder of the torch that's been passed to him. He picks up the mantle, walks back, and stands on the bank of the Jordan. What a pivotal moment in Elisha's life. He takes the cloak and rolls it up, just as he had seen Elijah do. He lifts his arm, just as he had seen Elijah do. Then, he swallows hard and gets ready, and he strikes the water of the Jordan.

The water parts, and Elisha crosses on dry ground. The mantle has been passed, the Spirit is alive in Elisha, and he is ready to be a torchbearer for God.

HISTORICAL CONTEXT

A Double Portion

Elisha's answer to Elijah's question can be confusing if we don't understand the historical context behind it. Elisha says, "Let me inherit a double portion of your spirit." This can sound a little greedy. It can almost sound as if he is saying, "Elijah, however much of the Holy Spirit you have, I want twice as much. I want twice as much power as you and I want to do twice as many miracles."

Sometimes people have taken this to mean that the Spirit can come in different percentages in different people. For example, "You might be filled with 23 percent of the Spirit, I'm 46 percent filled up, and Billy Graham is probably 99 percent filled with the Spirit." Is that what Elisha is communicating? It does not seem so.

Elisha is using classic inheritance language. Back in Deuteronomy 21:17 God said that the heir—the firstborn—is to receive a double portion of the inheritance. To ask for the double portion is to ask to be someone's heir. That's what it means here. The double portion is that which goes to the heir. Elisha even uses this explicit word: "Let me inherit it."

Elisha is not asking for two helpings of the Spirit. He's saying, "Elijah, I've watched your life and I've seen your ministry. I've witnessed your devotion and the difference you've made. I've seen how Israel is a different place because of your ministry. The power of Baal worship has been broken because of your devotion and courage. I want to continue following in your steps, even after you are gone."

NARRATIVE ON LIFE | God's Work through Elisha

The God of Elijah has become the God of Elisha. This prophet goes on to have an extraordinary life that parallels Elijah's in many ways. He dictates battle strategies to the kings of Israel and Judah. He challenges the most powerful people in society with utter fearlessness. He helps a powerless, impoverished widow in a time of need. These are all things Elijah has done. Elisha has learned well at the feet of the master prophet, and along the way, he became a great prophet as well.

3. Elisha Carries the Flame

NARRATIVE ON THE TEXT | Don't Ask for Just a Few

SIGNIFICANT SCRIPTURE

2 Kings 4:1-7

Elisha encounters a woman who is in dire straits. Her sons are about to be sold into slavery. She is deeply in debt and has nowhere to go and no one to help her. So, she runs to Elisha. This woman is sure she has nothing of any value. But, Elisha poses a provocative question. He asks the woman if she has *anything at all* in her house. Her response is, "Your servant has nothing there at all except a little oil."

Elisha tells her that God will miraculously give all the oil she needs so she can sell it and pay off all her debts. His words bring hope that she and her sons will have all they need to live. But, Elisha asks her to do something specific. He has her gather as many jars as she can find. She is to go around to all of her neighbors and ask for every container they can spare. Elisha speaks these words: "Don't ask for just a few."

LIFE APPLICATION | A Big-Jar God!

God gives this widow, her sons, all of Israel, and all who read the Bible an unforgettable lesson. "Don't ask for just a few. If you give God a few jars; he'll fill a few. When we give him a lot of jars, he'll fill a lot." In this story we learn the lesson that our God is a big-jar God! He has the resources to fill every jar we bring to him.

God comes to us today and asks, "What do you have?" We may look and say, "Nothing!" But God says, "Look closer." If all we have is a little oil, God can multiply it and provide all we need. The same God who gave manna in the desert, who delivered meat special delivery by ravens, who sent angels to bring cake in the desert, can fill our jars also. We need to look at the little we have, place it in the hands of our big-jar God, and watch what he can do with it!

I have learned to place myself before God every day as a vessel to be filled with His Holy Spirit. He has filled me with the blessed assurance that He, as the everlasting God, has guaranteed His own work in me.

ANDREW MURRAY

SIGNIFICANT SCRIPTURE

2 Kings 6:8-23

NARRATIVE ON THE TEXT | Who's the Mole?

Another amazing story about Elisha's ministry and character occurs when the king of Aram is trying to kill the king of Israel. He makes many attempts to assassinate Joram, king of Israel, but every time he makes a plan, God tells Elisha, who in turn passes the information on to the king of Israel. So, every time the king of Aram advances, Joram escapes.

The king of Aram starts to get angry. He can't figure out why the king of Israel is always one step ahead of him. So, the king of Aram starts to ask some questions, "Who's the mole? Where's the leak? How can Joram know my plans before I execute them?" He is sure there is someone in his camp that is working as a double agent.

His leaders assure him that there is not a mole. They tell him that Elisha has the power to know the very words the king speaks in the privacy of his own bedroom. The king of Aram thus decides that the only way he will ever get to Joram, king of Israel, is to take out Elisha first. So, again, a prophet of God finds out what it is like to be on the death list of a king.

The king of Aram finds out that Elisha has gone to the city of Dothan, so he brings in his army and surrounds the city. They are there for one reason—to capture and assassinate Elisha. Just think about it, one man demands the attack of a whole army.

The next morning Elisha's servant gets up and looks outside of the city. There is a human wall surrounding the city on every side. There were soldiers, chariots, and a military machine that would send fear into the heart of any ordinary man. But Elisha is not an ordinary man, because he serves an extraordinary God. When Elisha's servant looks and sees their situation, all he can see is the apparent power and impenetrable position of the army surrounding the city. When Elisha looks, he sees something very different, so he says to his servant: "Don't be afraid. . . . Those who are with us are more than those who are with them" (2 Kings 6:16).

INTERPRETIVE INSIGHT | Spiritual Realities Beyond the Physical

How do you think Elisha's words sound to his servant as he looks and sees the army surrounding the city? You can almost hear him saying, "How many are with us? Two." And then looking outside the city again, he says, "How many are with them? I can't count that high!" He must have wondered what Elisha is talking about. How can Elisha say that those who are with them are more than the ones who surround the city?

But then, Elisha prays for God to open his servant's eyes and help him see beyond the physical world to the spiritual reality. When God opens the eyes of Elijah's servant, he sees a radically different reality. The hills all around Dothan are full of horses and chariots of fire. The army of God surrounds the army of Aram, and the angels also surround Elisha. Human eyes showed that the odds were in favor of the king of Aram. Spiritual eyes reveal that the King of heaven is with Elisha—and the victory always goes to God!

LIFE APPLICATION | Open My Eyes!

Many followers of Christ need to hear the words: "Don't be afraid. Those who are with us are more than those who are with them." Whatever we face—problems, challenges, difficulties, fears, or worries—we all have times we need to shift our eyes from earthly to heavenly realities. Sometimes we need to ask God to show us what is happening in the heavenly realms so that we can walk with courage in this life.

At other times, we need to pray for faith to believe what our eyes can't see. Like the servant of Elisha, we need to learn that those who are with us, when we stand with the Lord, are always more than those who are with them.

NARRATIVE ON THE TEXT | Shocking Compassion

There is a postscript to the story of Elisha's servant learning that "those who are with us are more than those who are with them." Elisha prays for God to blind the entire army. Once they are blind, Elisha leads them into the capital city of Israel. This is the home city of King Joram, who the king of Aram has been plotting to kill. Once they are in the city and surrounded by the army of Israel, God opens their eyes and they realize that they are in big trouble.

NEW TESTAMENT CONNECTION | He Who Is In You

The lesson learned by Elisha's servant is reinforced many times and in many ways in the New Testament. Two passages that hit this theme hard are:

> You, dear children, are from God and have overcome them, because the one who is in you is greater than the one who is in the world. (1 John 4:4)

> Finally, be strong in the Lord and in his mighty power. Put on the full armor of God so that you can take your stand against the devil's schemes. For our struggle is not against flesh and blood, but against the rulers, against the authorities, against the powers of this dark world and against the spiritual forces of evil in the heavenly realms. Therefore put on the full armor of God, so that when the day of evil comes, you may be able to stand your ground, and after you have done everything, to stand. (Ephesians 6:10–13)

Over and over the Scriptures remind us that there is a spiritual reality beyond the physical world we see day in and day out. But in the battles we face, God is always able to bring the victory.

PAUSE FOR PRAYER

As you close in prayer, ask God to make each person a passer of the torch. Thank God for those who serve as volunteers with humble and committed hearts. Pray for your church to be deeply committed to pass on the spiritual legacy God has given you from those who have gone before you.

The king of Israel asks Elisha if he should execute the entire army. Elisha says, "I have a better idea! Let's have them sit down and let's serve them a feast!" And that is exactly what they do. Elisha exercises shocking compassion and grace. The postscript to the postscript is that the army of Aram stops raiding and harassing the people of Israel. Is that any surprise?

LIFE APPLICATION | Growing in Compassion

Elisha shocks the people of Israel, the king of Israel, and certainly the army of Aram. When is the last time someone was shocked by the compassion they saw exhibited in your life? When is the last time you exercised radical compassion that revealed the deep love of God for people who don't deserve forgiveness and grace? Why not take time to think of someone who could use a dose of compassion and then ask God to help you be the one to deliver it.

CREATIVE MESSAGE IDEA | A Time to Bless!

You may want to close this message by taking time to bless and affirm those in your church who have committed themselves to humble volunteer service. There are countless ways this happens in the church, but identify some of the examples of this and celebrate those people who have heard the call and followed God into a life of serving. Remind them that the heart of Jesus beats loudly through their example no matter where they serve:

- in the nursery
- as a children's teacher
- in youth ministry
- in prayer ministry
- in counseling and visitation
- on a church board
- in women's or men's ministry
- as a missionary at home or abroad
- and the list goes on and on!

SESSION 3

Amos: How to Measure a Life

DEUTERONOMY 24:12–22; AMOS 1:1–4:3; 5:21–24; 7:1–9

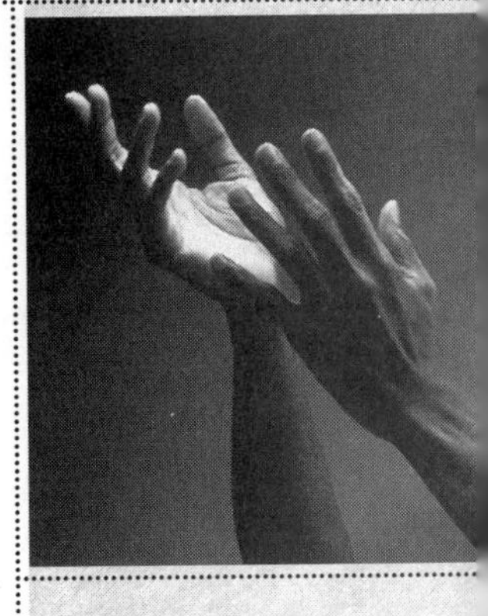

The Heart of the MESSAGE

In a critical time of Israel's history, God spoke through Amos to give the people a serious wake-up call. The time of Amos's ministry was one of great affluence and peace. Not since the days of Solomon could the people remember a time when things were going so well in their nation. The economy was strong, and those who were rich just seemed to be getting richer! It seemed everyone was reaping the benefits of this season of God's blessing—except those who were poor.

As we read the book of Amos, it quickly becomes apparent that the rich were indeed getting richer. At the same time, however, the poor were getting poorer and, in some ways, the wealth of the rich was being amassed at the expense of the poor and through unjust practices.

God intervenes and calls Amos to speak to the nation. He calls them to justice, righteousness, and compassion. God is deeply concerned for the plight of all those who are marginalized and calls his people to adopt a new attitude and lifestyle that reflect his care for the poor and oppressed.

This message has a great deal to say to those who live in affluence. The warnings and exhortations from Amos echo throughout the millennia and speak to the church and followers of Christ in our day. If we listen closely, we can hear the call from complacency to acts of justice and compassion.

Brief Message OUTLINE

1. Meeting Amos
2. Hearing Amos
3. The Message of Amos
4. The Warning and Challenge of Amos

The Heart of the MESSENGER

Anyone who lives in an affluent society can be tempted to consume more and express less compassion with each passing year. Followers of Jesus need to do a close lifestyle examination to be sure that they are living with a generous spirit, a heart of compassion, and eyes that are always open to the needs of the poor and the outcast. As a leader, take time to do a personal life examination. Invite the Holy Spirit to show you areas of your life and behaviors that might lead to injustice. Take all you have, and all you are, and place it before the Lord. Ask him to use these resources to bring glory to him and blessing to others.

1. Meeting Amos

NARRATIVE ON THE TEXT Meeting Amos

SIGNIFICANT SCRIPTURE
Amos 1-3

Amos lived and ministered around 750 B.C. He was *not* a professional prophet. Rather, he was a farmer. He took care of a few sheep and tended some fig trees. He was from a little town near Bethlehem called Tekoa, in the southern kingdom (Judah). One day, God called this man to leave his sheep and go proclaim God's word. God did not call Amos to preach in Judah, his hometown, but to go up to the northern kingdom (Israel) and preach there.

2. Hearing Amos

Interpretive Insight: When Things Are Going Great!

At the time that Amos is called to prophesy, the northern kingdom (Israel) is enjoying political success and economic prosperity unknown since the days of

CREATIVE MESSAGE IDEA Bold Words

What's the boldest thing you have ever said to somebody? What's the one statement you made that took more guts than you knew you had? What was it that moved you to a place of speaking with this level of boldness?

The Bible is filled with examples of people who spoke words of amazing boldness. Here are just a few examples.

(1) When David faced Goliath and this human tank threatened to give his flesh to the birds and animals of the field (and he meant this literally), this was David's response:

> "You come against me with sword and spear and javelin, but I come against you in the name of the LORD Almighty, the God of the armies of Israel, whom you have defied. This day the LORD will hand you over to me, and I'll strike you down and cut off your head. Today I will give the carcasses of the Philistine army to the birds of the air and the beasts of the earth, and the whole world will know that there is a God in Israel." (1 Samuel 17:45-46)

(2) When John the Baptist met the religious leaders of his day, this was his greeting:

> "You brood of vipers! Who warned you to flee from the coming wrath? Produce fruit in keeping with repentance. And do not think you can say to yourselves, 'We have Abraham as our father.' I tell you that out of these stones God can raise up children for Abraham. The ax is already at the root of the trees, and every tree that does not produce good fruit will be cut down and thrown into the fire." (Matthew 3:7-10)

(3) When the apostle Paul stood before King Agrippa and boldly presented the gospel, Agrippa asked this question: "Do you think that in such a short time you can persuade me to be a Christian?" Paul's response is heartfelt and incredibly bold:

> "Short time or long—I pray God that not only you but all who are listening to me today may become what I am, except for these chains." (Acts 26:29)

If you have someone in your church who can help you develop a short video, it might be fun to collect a number of short accounts of people telling about the most bold thing they ever said. These statements might be serious or humorous. You could show this brief video at the start of this section of the message.

Solomon. The people in the northern kingdom who have wealth are real happy with the way their lives are going. Investments are paying great interest and the market is strong, to put things in modern terms. If you have money to invest, you are sure to become even richer! God sends Amos to Samaria, the capital city of the northern kingdom. Samaria is the center of wealth and power in Israel—New York City and Washington, D.C., combined.

ON THE LIGHTER SIDE

Finding Amos

Invite people to turn to the book of Amos. If they seem to have a hard time finding this brief prophetic book tucked away in the Minor Prophets of the Old Testament, tell them that it is right before Obadiah. All they have to do is find Obadiah (a one-chapter book) and go back a book.

NARRATIVE ON THE TEXT

A Brilliant Set-Up!

When Amos shows up in Samaria and begins to preach, we can be confident that the people are wondering what the new prophet from Judah (the southern kingdom) will say. When they hear his opening words about judgment on Damascus, the capital city of the Aramean state, they are thrilled. The Arameans are a bitter enemy and a constant threat to Israel. All who hear will undoubtedly stop and wait to hear more. Their initial response would be, "I like this prophet! He must be from God because he is speaking against our enemies! I want to hear more from this new prophetic voice." In the Creative Message Idea below, however, you can see how Amos is setting up this people for some shocking news.

CREATIVE MESSAGE IDEA

Make Some Noise

In Old Testament days, when a prophet or preacher spoke, the people would often respond out loud to what was said. In other words, if they liked what they were hearing, they would cheer. If they were offended, they might hiss, boo, or even grind their teeth in anger. The message was interactive.

In each of the eight prophetic words to the nations, there are three movements.

1. It begins with the announcement of a nation that has pushed God too far. The people have placed the final straw on the camel's back and have crossed the line. So, God announces that judgment will be coming. At this point, the people may have responded with a gasp of amazement, a sigh of awe, or a cheer of affirmation.
2. Next is an unveiling of what the nation did that has pushed God over the edge. A specific sin, or list of sins, is recorded. At this point the people may have hissed, given a boo, or expressed great shock at the sins of the pagan nations around them.
3. Finally, there was a declaration of judgment on the nation. Amos expresses what God is going to do to this nation for their sin. At this, the people of Israel would be cheering, celebrating, giving high fives, and outwardly expressing their joy that their enemies are finally getting what they deserve!

As you read Amos 1:3–2:3, invite people to imagine they are the Israelites hearing these words for the first time. You may even want to have everyone stand as they listen. Invite them to respond, out loud, in a way they think reflects how the people of Israel would feel about what they are hearing. Their bitter enemies, who have persecuted, attacked, and oppressed them for years, are now getting judged by God. You may want to use the visual prompters provided in the Power Point CD in the OTC packet.

When you get to 2:4–5, the judgment on Judah (the southern kingdom), pause for a moment. Remind those gathered that Amos is from Judah, and now he is prophesying against his own people. Remind them that Judah and Israel are in a time of regular conflict and war. Then, read Amos 2:4–5 and invite people to respond as they feel Israel would respond.

At this point the people of Israel would be applauding and cheering, and if those hearing the message get the point of this exercise, they will be applauding and cheering too! Israel is sure that they are righteous and loved by God and that every other nation is evil and deserves God's judgment. They are thrilled to hear that God is finally going to step in and punish the nations for their sin. This was all good news to Israel.

But, what comes next shocks them all!

Ask for complete silence. Ask everyone to imagine what is going through the minds and hearts of the people of Israel as they hear these words—the words of Amos 2:6-16.

WORD STUDY

"For Three Sins and for Four"

When Amos begins preaching, he uses a specific formula as he speaks words of judgment on eight different nations. Each time he speaks about a nation, he begins with these words:

> This is what the LORD says:
> "*For three sins* of [city/territory name],
> *even for four*, I will not turn back my wrath. (Amos 1:3, 6, 9, 11, 13; 2:1, 4, 6)

Then Amos goes on to tell how each nation has offended God and pushed his patience to a breaking point. The phraseology used here, "For three sins and for four," has specific meaning. This is a formal pronouncement of judgment!

In English we might say something like, "That was the straw that broke the camel's back." The words "For three sins and for four" is the Hebrew way of saying, "The camel is in a full-body cast. The people have gone too far. Judgment is coming!"

3. The Message of Amos

INTERPRETIVE INSIGHT

How You Treat the Poor Really Matters

When we listen to the words Amos speaks about Israel, it almost sounds as if God sees them as one of his enemies. God appears to lump Israel together with the Arameans, Philistines, Edomites, and the other nations of the world. And that is exactly what God is doing through the words of Amos. He is charging Israel with living as though they were God's enemies.

What's the last straw?

What is the act that sets God's teeth on edge?

What is the third and fourth sin that pushes God over the limit?

Amos is crystal clear on this issue. The sin of Israel is the way they are treating the poor. God has given them abundance and plenty of resources. But instead of helping the poor and oppressed, they are hoarding it all for themselves. They are living in luxury while poverty exists all around them, and they don't even care!

This is amazing. Amos charges Ammon with ripping open the wombs of pregnant women (Amos 1:13) and the Philistines with taking whole communities captive and selling them to Edom (1:6). But these sins are not nearly as bad in God's eyes as what his own people are doing—trampling the heads of the poor among them and denying justice to the oppressed (2:6–7).

LIFE APPLICATION

Seeking Balance

God does not say that the people of Israel don't worship enough. He doesn't say that they don't know the Scriptures. He doesn't say a whole lot of things we might have expected him to say. He says, "My heart is broken over the way my people hoard their resources and neglect the poor while they claim to follow and know me."

HISTORICAL CONTEXT

The Writing Prophets

All through the Bible we see bold words expressed. Amos is no exception. He speaks some of the boldest words in the Bible. In these chapters Amos speaks to the enemies of Israel, to Judah, and then to his own people!

Amos is probably the earliest of what were called the "writing prophets." These are the prophets who have books in their names that contain the story of their lives or the messages God called them to speak. There were other prophets before them, like Elijah and Elisha, but they were not writing prophets. Their stories are recorded by others in the flow of the Old Testament narrative. But Amos, as well as many other prophets, wrote down their messages, which are recorded in the latter part of the Old Testament.

God is deeply concerned about our worship. He cares very much that we know the teaching of Scripture. God wants us to attend church services and share in life-giving fellowship among his people. But this is not the whole story! When we truly worship God, our hearts are captured by the things that matter to God, and God cares about the poor, the oppressed, and the outcast. When we study the Bible, we should follow what it teaches. This means we must learn from Amos and begin to act in ways that will bring justice for those who are marginalized. God longs to see a balance in the lives of his followers. Spirit-led worship should lead to passionate service and compassionate acts of justice.

Many years earlier, God had spoken through Moses to teach the people the importance of compassion and justice. He said:

> Do not deprive the alien or the fatherless of justice, or take the cloak of the widow as a pledge. Remember that you were slaves in Egypt and the LORD your God redeemed you from there. That is why I command you to do this. (Deuteronomy 24:17–18)

The people of Israel were always to look back and remember that God had showed them compassion when they were oppressed in Egypt, and they were to live with care for those who were oppressed, outcast, and needy. The community established by God should be marked by compassion and justice.

INTERPRETIVE INSIGHT | The Heart of God for the Needy

In Deuteronomy 24:17 we see three groups of people specifically listed. They are the:

- alien
- fatherless
- widow

Since Israel experienced oppression in Egypt, they should be particularly sensitive to those who were in a similar situation. And, since they knew the heart of God, they should extend the same kind of grace and justice that God gives. But just to make sure, God made it explicit.

PAUSE FOR PRAYER

Search Our Hearts, O God!

You can use the prayer below, or your own prayer, to invite the Holy Spirit to speak to each heart through the words of Amos.

> Holy Spirit of God, search our hearts today. Spare us from the folly of listening to your Word and judging others by what we hear. Please help each of us see where injustice rules in our heart and life. Help us see where we are in need of conviction, challenge, and change.
>
> We confess that we can be quick to judge others while we absolve ourselves of any responsibility for our choices and actions. Teach us justice and change our hearts and lives to reflect what you want for us and the world we live in. Spirit of God, speak to us in power and open our ears to hear, our hearts to receive, and our lives to be transformed!
>
> We pray this in the name of Jesus, Amen.

SIGNIFICANT SCRIPTURE

Deuteronomy 24:17-22

CREATIVE VIDEO ELEMENT

(VHS or DVD)

Personal Story: St. Charles Place (4:40 min.)
This interview segment shows the impact we can have on the world when people reach out to the needy.

> When you are harvesting in your field and you overlook a sheaf, do not go back to get it. Leave it for the *alien*, the *fatherless* and the *widow*, so that the LORD your God may bless you in all the work of your hands. When you beat the olives from your trees, do not go over the branches a second time. Leave what remains for the *alien*, the *fatherless* and the *widow*. When you harvest the grapes in your vineyard, do not go over the vines again. Leave what remains for the *alien*, the *fatherless* and the *widow*. Remember that you were slaves in Egypt. That is why I command you to do this. (Deuteronomy 24:19–22)

There is no way to miss the refrain in this passage. Moreover, this same concern is found throughout the Old Testament. God cares about those who cannot care for themselves, and he expects his followers to care too.

We choose to be poor for the love of God. In the service of the poorest of the poor, we are feeding the hungry Christ, clothing the naked Christ, and giving shelter to the homeless Christ.

MOTHER TERESA OF CALCUTTA

LIFE APPLICATION | The Marginalized of Our Day

Every society and generation must face the reality that there are groups that can be easily marginalized. In the days of Amos, as we have seen, it was the alien, the fatherless, and the widow. Our responsibility is to discern where these groups exist in our society and then seek to extend the compassion and tender love of God for these people. We need to seek justice for those who are treated with injustice. The particular groups of people may change with varied contexts, but

HISTORICAL CONTEXT | Garment Taken in Pledge

One of the accusations God levels at the people through the words of Amos is this: "They lie down beside every altar on garments taken in pledge" (2:8). In those days garments were often taken as collateral from the poor. For those who lived on the ragged edge of poverty, sometimes their only possession was a cloak or garment that they wore during the day and used as a blanket at night. If they needed a small loan or if they owed something to another person, this garment could be taken until they paid back what was owed. God strictly commanded, however, that any garment taken in pledge had to be given back at nightfall so the poor person would not freeze.

In Deuteronomy 24:12–13 we read:

> If the man is poor, do not go to sleep with his pledge in your possession. Return his cloak to him by sunset so that he may sleep in it. Then he will thank you, and it will be regarded as a righteous act in the sight of the LORD your God.

But the wealthy people of Israel were taking garments in pledge and failing to give them back at nightfall. On top of that, they were taking these garments into pagan temples, drinking wine, and laying down on them as part of their idolatrous revelry.

Amos points these out as glaring acts of injustice, so that the judgment of God is coming, and you can be sure the people of Israel are not cheering anymore.

there will always be marginalized people groups, and God will always expect his children to seek them out and extend justice and mercy toward them.

The marginalized could be persons of color, immigrants, senior citizens, teenagers, people with physical or mental disabilities, or some minority group, but every society that has ever existed has them. It is so important that we understand the heart of God toward these people and take actions that communicate God's love for the outcasts.

SIGNIFICANT SCRIPTURE

Deuteronomy 24:12–13

NARRATIVE ON LIFE | How God Sees a Society

God says he will judge a society by the way it treats marginalized people. God makes it unmistakably clear that he takes it on himself to be the protector of the weak and outcast in a society. Anybody who neglects them neglects him. Anybody who oppresses them oppresses him.

> He who is kind to the poor lends to the LORD,
> and he will reward him for what he has done. (Proverbs 19:17)
>
> A father to the fatherless, a defender of widows,
> is God in his holy dwelling. (Psalm 68:5)

Throughout the Old Testament God expresses his heart toward the marginalized and invites us to join in his commitment to bring love and justice to those who often don't receive it.

God, being who he is, cannot cease to be what he is. He cannot act out of character with himself. Because he is faithful, he is faithful in all his actions.

MILLIE STAMM

HISTORICAL CONTEXT | The Alien, the Fatherless, and the Widow

Why was God so concerned for these three groups of people?

Aliens were those people who immigrated into the land of Israel. They were not ethnic Israelites, so they did not have the same rights and privileges as the people of Israel. The *fatherless* were those who had been orphaned and had no one to provide for them or to look out for them. The *widows* were women who had lost their husbands; in the patriarchal society in which they lived, these people were without legal and political power or economic means.

In our day these are called marginalized people. They are the groups that will most likely be forgotten, mistreated, oppressed, and broken if someone does not speak up. God is concerned for them because they need someone to help them, to speak for them, to love them.

ILLUSTRATION | The Feet of Mother Teresa

A story is told of a man who spent time serving with Mother Teresa in Calcutta. Once, while working at her side, he noticed that her feet were badly misshapen. This troubled him, though he did not ask her about it. Later on, he asked somebody in the community about her feet.

He was told that among the poor there are never enough shoes. Mother Teresa always insisted that when shoes were donated, the best pairs always be given away to the most poor. She always took the worst for herself—whatever was left over. As the years passed, her feet became badly deformed. For Mother Teresa, consistent acts of compassion for the poor cost her something. Compassion always does.

INTERPRETIVE INSIGHT | A Look at What Is Really of Worth

Amos hits the people of Israel right where they live. He lets them know that God sees their greed and devaluation of human life. To many of these people a human life was worth as much as a pair of sandals. In many cases, people valued a pair of their shoes more than a person.

Over time, many of the people became so wealthy that they built winter and summer homes. They invested all their money in creating luxurious places to live and had nothing left to give the poor. God lets the people know that their opulent lifestyle and hard hearts will lead to their downfall. God speaks through Amos and says, "I will tear down the winter house along with the summer house; the houses adorned with ivory will be destroyed and the mansions will be demolished."

NEW TESTAMENT CONNECTION

The Least of These

Jesus affirms the heart of God for those who are outcast. He too speaks of the hungry, imprisoned, sick, and marginalized and is emphatic that how we treat these people reflects how we see God. Listen to his words: "I tell you the truth, whatever you did for one of the least of these brothers of mine, you did for me" (Matthew 25:40). A close study of Matthew 25:31-46 will affirm that he has the same heart toward the outcast and the needy as God the Father expresses throughout the Old Testament.

SIGNIFICANT SCRIPTURE

Amos 2:6 and 3:15

HISTORICAL CONTEXT | Archaeological Evidence

In the days of Amos there was a shocking disparity between the rich and the poor. Archaeologists have confirmed this through various finds over the years. Back when Canaan was first populated, God gave equal property to all the tribes. Everybody lived at a fairly modest level. Archaeological evidence shows that houses from the tenth century B.C. are all fairly similar. But by the time we reach Amos's day (the eighth century B.C.), archaeologists find evidence of enormous mansions for the rich and miserable hovels for the poor.

ILLUSTRATION | Getting a Little Justice

The first Mayor Daley of Chicago was famous for many things. One of them was his great self-confidence and brashness. He was approached once by one of his speechwriters who said, "Mayor Daley, I'm not making enough money." Daley's response was, "I'm not going to give you any more money. It ought to be enough that you work for a great American hero like me." That was the end of the discussion, or so he thought.

Several weeks later, Daley was on his way to give a speech. He was famous for never reading his speeches before he got up to deliver them. In this case, he got up to give a speech to a large group of veterans on a Veteran's Day celebration. It was getting national press coverage.

Daley began the speech, and as he delivered it, he was quite impressed with how eloquent and passionate it was. He talked about how everybody had forgotten the veterans. Then he assured them, "I remember and I care." He said, "Today I am proposing a seventeen-point program—national, state, and city wide—to take care of the veterans of our country."

By this time everyone was on the edge of their seat. They wanted to find out what he was going to say next. They were excited to hear about this elaborate and expansive plan to care for the veterans. The truth is, at this point Mayor Daley was pretty interested himself. He couldn't wait to find out what he was going to say next. So, he turned the page over and all it said was, "You're on your own now, you great American hero."

This story has been floating around for years. It might be true or it might be apocryphal, but it is a great example of someone getting the justice he deserved. We all love a story when wrongs are made right and injustice is stamped out.

INTERPRETIVE INSIGHT | Do You Think God Fails to Notice?

The people of Israel knew the words of Deuteronomy that called them to justice and compassion. They had simply decided they did not want to follow this teaching. It almost seems as if they believed God had forgotten or failed to notice what they were doing. They had reached a point where they felt they were entitled to all the money and power they could gather. In their blindness they betrayed God's vision for a just, compassionate society.

So Amos says to them, "Do you think God was just joking when he gave his law? Do you think God doesn't see what's going on? Do you think God doesn't care about these people he has defended for so long? Do you really think that you can take all of your resources, which all come from God's hand, and use them in whatever way you choose to just enrich yourself?" The people had become so blind to the plight of the poor and so numb to the cry of the oppressed that they actually were getting mad at God for not giving them even more.

NARRATIVE ON THE TEXT | A Word to the Women of Israel

SIGNIFICANT SCRIPTURE
Amos 4:1–3

Amos uses any tool he can to try to wake up people from their complacency. He gives a specific word to the women who are living in opulent wealth:

> Hear this word, you cows of Bashan on Mount Samaria,
> you women who oppress the poor and crush the needy
> and say to your husbands, "Bring us some drinks!"
> (Amos 4:1)

Ouch!

Amos is calling the wives of the wealthy and powerful "cows of Bashan." Do you think they feel complimented by this? Bashan was a fertile area. The cows there were famous for being well fed and large! That's why he calls the women "cows of Bashan."

This is not just random name-calling. Think about the nature of a cow. Cows are not notable for their good works. Cows are just a walking appetite. They actually have four stomachs and are eating machines. They consume—it's what they do best! The only question they ask is, "Where can I get more?"

NARRATIVE ON LIFE | The "Cows of Bashan Syndrome"

We live in a society that often encourages us to live like cows of Bashan. Our media culture wants us to become walking appetites for money, food, and pleasure. The questions many of us ask are:

How can I get a bigger house?

How can I get a larger income?

How can I drive a newer car?

How can I have greater sexual pleasure?

How can I be more attractive?

Our culture has become effective in producing cows of Bashan. This reality should cause every follower of Jesus to evaluate his or her life and motives closely.

The deeper problem for the people of Israel was that they made no connection between their treatment of the poor and their relationship with God. We can fall into this same pattern. We can worship, give our offerings, and feel pretty good about ourselves, but our hearts might still be hard toward those who are poor and outcast. God wants to get into our hearts and help us feel as he does for the poor. Then, he wants to transform our lifestyle and teach us to be generous toward the marginalized and needy.

ILLUSTRATION | The Games We Play

There are many board games that children play as they are growing up. Think for a moment about Monopoly. The goal of this game is to gain all of the property and wealth possible. In doing so, it demands that a player take money from others, and if necessary, send them to the poorhouse. Another classic game is Risk, a game whose goal is a little broader than Monopoly. In Risk, the goal is to conquer the whole world. To win, a player must go to war and defeat every other player until their players cover the face of the earth.

This is not meant to be a criticism of these board games. It is simply an observation. The games we play growing up can reinforce the idea that gaining wealth and power is the goal of life. God has a very different vision for us to see.

4. The Warning and Challenge of Amos

INTERPRETIVE INSIGHT | When Injustice Meets Worship

Imagine the shock waves going through the crowd when they hear Amos claiming that God says he hates their worship and religious observance. They have never heard such a thing. What can this mean? Amos cries out:

SIGNIFICANT SCRIPTURE
Amos 5:21-24

> I hate, I despise your religious feasts;
> I cannot stand your assemblies.
> Even though you bring me burnt offerings and grain
> offerings,
> I will not accept them.
> Though you bring choice fellowship offerings,
> I will have no regard for them.
> Away with the noise of your songs!
> I will not listen to the music of your harps. (Amos 5:21–23)

God is saying to the people, "Your worship and your lives can't be separated!" They want to hoard wealth, trample on the poor, oppress the weak, and then show up for church as if God doesn't notice any of their behavior. God is clear that life does not work this way. Injustice and authentic worship cannot coexist in the life of someone who follows Jesus.

LIFE APPLICATION | A Call to Justice

In one of the great statements in all the Bible, Amos unveils the heart of God:

> But let justice roll on like a river,
> righteousness like a never-failing stream! (Amos 5:24)

SIGNIFICANT SCRIPTURE

Amos 7:1-9

God is saying, "Let justice and compassion flow out of your lives. Don't sit there eating vast amounts of food at your religious feasts while the poor are starving to death outside your door, and don't congratulate yourselves on how much you love me. It is time for the earth to be covered with rivers of righteousness and justice, and my people are the ones I will use to make this dream a reality."

As followers of Jesus we need to identify the ways God can use us to let justice and righteousness flow across this earth. Local churches need to be places where the marginalized know they are welcomed and loved. We even need to go a step further and go out to find those who are outcast and extend the loving mercy of God to them.

If your church has ministries that reach out to the poor, the oppressed, and the marginalized, you may want to introduce these at this time.

WORD STUDY

Plumb Line

In ancient days, a plumb line was a standard tool for a builder. It was a very simple tool that was used to be sure a wall was built straight up and down. All it took to make a plumb line was a piece of string, a rock, and gravity.

A builder would hold a string, tie a stone to the end, and let the weight of a stone pull it straight toward the ground. This string would be exactly straight. It could be held up against a wall to see if it was built with integrity. If the wall was straight, or plumb, it could stand. If the plumb line showed that the wall was leaning one way or the other, it would often be torn down and rebuilt.

NARRATIVE ON THE TEXT | Three Pictures of Judgment

God give Amos three images, three pictures, of coming judgment. First, God threatens to send locusts. In an agricultural society, a locust swarm meant devastation to the economy and the ecology. Amos cries out, "God, don't do it! Your people can't survive," and God relents. Next, God says he is going to send fire on the land. Again Amos pleads for the nation and says, "Don't do it! It will destroy your people." Once again, God relents. Finally, God gives Amos a third image of judgment. This picture seems less threatening, but it is still shocking. God gives him a vision of a wall and a plumb line.

LIFE APPLICATION | How Do We Measure Our Lives?

We don't live in a plumb-line society. In our world, we like to measure ourselves by comparing ourselves to others. We don't like unchanging standards. We can always find somebody who is worse than us, greedier, and further away from God's standards. It's tempting to try to evade God's Word and standards by

ON THE LIGHTER SIDE | Plumb Is Plumb

A wall is either true to plumb or it is not. Carpenters, if you notice, are not really into relativism. They never say things like, "You know, you have your plumb and I have my plumb. We all have our own plumbs really, and if our plumbs should meet, that's a beautiful thing, but if they don't, that's beautiful too." Or, "Don't complain to me if you think your house isn't in plumb, because maybe it's not in plumb for you, but it's in plumb for me." Or, "Don't inflict your plumb on my plumb. We all have our own plumbs." Plumb doesn't work that way.

comparing ourselves to other people or to society as a whole. We can do this in many areas of life:

- *Generosity:* We can say, "My heart's generous. I want to be generous. I just don't have very much money right now. Things are kind of tight. Someday, I'll have more money and then I'll help take care of people who are in need." But for now, we go on spending every dime we have on ourselves.
- *Serving:* We can say, "I'm really busy right now. I'd love to serve people who are in need, but I can't fit it into my schedule. Maybe when I have more time and get on top of things, then I will serve those in need." But, our schedule never seems to open up, and serving never fits into our day planner.
- *Reaching out:* We can say, "I'd love to form a relationship with somebody of a different ethnicity or in a different culture. I'd love to do that. I really want to be part of God's solution to breaking down the walls that divide us, but it involves taking risks, and I am not up for that. I will wait for someone else to reach out to me, then maybe I can respond instead of initiate." But time passes and the walls grow higher and higher.

We can measure our lives by comparing ourselves, but God does not. He sets a standard that is radically different than the constantly changing world in which we live. We need to look to his Word, discover his standard, and then ask him for the strength to grow in our devotion to live with the justice, righteousness, and compassion that marks the heart of God.

God says, "I will measure my people by the one standard that counts. And it's a real simple standard. Are there hungry people? Feed them. Are there sick people? Help them. Are there oppressed people? Stick up for them. Are there lonely widows? Visit them. Are there uneducated children? Teach them. Are there people who get rejected because of the color of their skin? Befriend them."

CREATIVE MESSAGE IDEA | A Wall and a Plumb Line

To illustrate the concept of a wall being plumb or straight, you may want to have a small section of a wall built where you will be teaching. Also have some twine and a stone (about the size of a fist). While you are talking about a plumb line you can make one. Then, as you talk about how it is used, you can show it. You may want the section of wall to be out of plumb so you can illustrate how God saw the people of Israel. They were an unstable and dangerous wall; they would have to be knocked over before they could be rebuilt.

ILLUSTRATION | When Theory Meets Real Need

This is a story about a real person who encountered real need. His name was Frank. He was a lawyer in Miami. His wife talked him into going on a mission trip to the Dominican Republic, and he reluctantly agreed. He really thought he would do some scuba diving and get some R & R. What happened was different than he ever dreamed.

One afternoon Frank and his wife found themselves with a doctor friend of theirs. They were on the third floor of a five-story building totally unprepared for what they were about to see. The building was supposed to be a kind of an orphanage. They walked into a room, and immediately they began reeling from the stench of human waste. In that one room they saw dozens of children. Some had cerebral palsy. Others had Down's syndrome. Their doctor friend told them that most of these children had been thrown out like garbage. They were the ones Amos called the "aliens, widows, and orphans." They were society's outcasts.

Frank saw a boy about eight years old kept in a cage three feet tall, three feet long, and three feet wide. He asked why this boy was kept in a cage. He was told the boy was hyperactive and he was in there because it was the only way to control him. No one knew his name. He was like a nameless animal in a cage. He lived among seventy-five naked, deformed, dehydrated, starving orphans. The stench was so bad, he could barely breathe.

This place had no running water, no air conditioning, no working toilets, broken windows, decaying walls, and exposed electrical wiring. That was the only world these seventy-five children knew.

Frank said that when they first got involved, the children would take turns eating. One child would eat on Monday. And then, because there wasn't enough food to go around, that child wouldn't eat again until Wednesday. On the weekends no one received anything to eat at all. A bath consisted of pouring a cup of water on the child. Most of the children lay on the floor, chained to the beds or huddled in cages. They were trapped inside their bodies, unable to communicate, untouched by the outside world, craving for someone to see them, for someone to hold them, for someone to love them. Every single one of them was malnourished and dehydrated. Many of them were about to die.

CREATIVE MESSAGE IDEA | Project Child Help

The Power Point presentation has some pictures of Project Child Help. As the pictures are showing, read these words:

God said, "I'm a father to the fatherless."

What do you think seeing this does to the heart of God?

Jesus said, "As you have done it to the least of these, you have done it to me."

Frank and his wife, Lori, prayed and felt led to start a venture called Project Child Help. They run it out of their garage. They recruit doctors and nurses—everybody they can—to visit the Dominican Republic with them to help the children who are in need. They collect everything they can. Every time Frank has a vacation, he spends it taking 5,000 pounds of medicine, food, and clothes to the orphanage. American Airlines found out what he was doing, and they ship all the supplies there for free. And now, three years later, there's a little group of children who eat three times a day and who get bathed every day, because Frank and Lori have hired caretakers to be with them.

The lives of these children have dramatically changed because this couple took God's Word seriously. They were willing to go someplace for a couple of days and have their heart broken open by things that break the heart of God. Then, this couple had the courage to take their resources and place them in the hands of God.

PAUSE FOR PRAYER

How Can This Be?

Pray for those who have been swept up into the "cows of Bashan" frenzy of our culture. Ask God to help each person see a new vision of what life can really mean. Pray for those who are seeking to do justice and let righteousness flow like a river. Ask God to bring them joy and strength to continue moving forward. Finally, pray for the local church to grow in a commitment to accomplish God's justice in a world that so desperately needs to see God's love modeled in our actions.

NARRATIVE ON LIFE

The Difference God Can Make Through One Person

You never know the difference one human being can make. One man—a shepherd named Amos, a collector of figs—had a huge impact on his generation. One couple, who let God get inside of their hearts, is now being used by God to touch the lives of hundreds of children. You never know the difference one person can make. But God does.

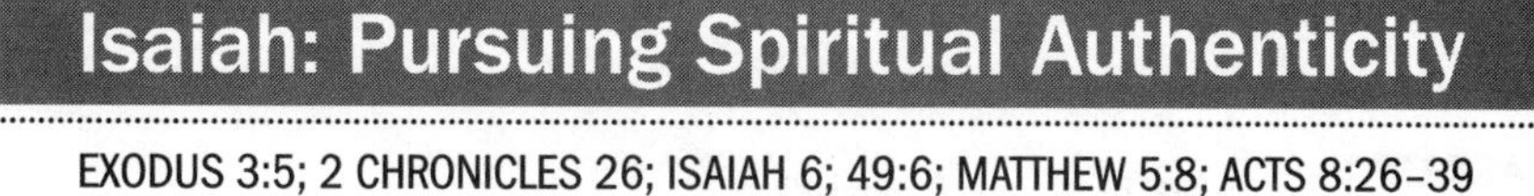

EXODUS 3:5; 2 CHRONICLES 26; ISAIAH 6; 49:6; MATTHEW 5:8; ACTS 8:26–39

The Heart of the **MESSAGE**

God invites Isaiah into a staggering place of worship. Isaiah sees God, and he is never the same. He learns that true and authentic worship has a price tag. It will cost us all we have and all we are. When we see God in the glory of his holiness, we enter worship as it was meant to be.

No more halfhearted songs, sleepy prayers, and leftovers in the offering plate. The radiance of God's holiness invites us to place our hearts and lives on the altar and to echo the words of Isaiah, "Here am I. Send me."

The Heart of the **MESSENGER**

We will never learn spiritual authenticity until we come to the throne of God. In the light of his holiness all pretense, facades, and playacting melt away. We learn to be authentic, who we really are, before God's throne.

As you prepare your heart to bring this message, spend time at the throne of God. Speak with him in prayer. Sing to him. Meditate on his Word. Meet with God and ask the Holy Spirit to remove any attitudes or actions that are inauthentic. Ask God to help you see his holiness and to transform you through his presence.

Brief Message **OUTLINE**

1. The Context: Uzziah's Death
2. The Confrontation: Seeing God
3. The Conversion: Changed by God
4. The Call: Led by God

1. The Context: Uzziah's Death

SIGNIFICANT SCRIPTURE
Isaiah 6:1-8

NARRATIVE ON LIFE | Cost Free or Costly?

There are actually people who take the time to study things like channel surfing. There really are! Their studies tell us that habitual channel surfing has some negative effects:

- It decreases our attention span.
- It decreases our ability to pay sustained attention—to learn.
- It increases our sense of isolation and passivity.

The obvious question is, if channel surfing sucks away so many hours of our life and gives so little back, why do we do it? The answer, of course, is because it doesn't cost us anything. It's easy to do. There's no effort involved.

In a world where channel surfing has become a national pastime, followers of Jesus need to be careful that we don't take a channel-surfing attitude into our worship experiences. In Isaiah 6 we see a model of worship that is anything but passive! In this passage of the Bible we discover that worship is active and costly. Authentic worship always demands an investment.

ILLUSTRATION | You Are Here

Every person who is gathered to hear this message on Isaiah has paid a price already. It takes a commitment to come to a worship service. Some people drove a long distance. Others exerted great energy motivating children to get ready for church. Still others felt emotionally depleted and spent every ounce of their emotional energy reserve just to get dressed and show up. On some level, every person gathered has already made an investment to gather with God's people for worship. The simple fact that you are here and are listening to the message is a reminder that worship costs something—every time.

CREATIVE MESSAGE IDEA | An Interactive Message

In this message it will be helpful if you can weave in some worship experiences with the teaching. There are worship suggestions at two points during the message, including songs, Scriptures, prayers, and silence. Let people know, from the beginning of the message, that this will be an active and participatory worship experience. Invite them to engage and be active in worship.

INTERPRETIVE INSIGHT | Sustained Attention

The costly nature of worship goes beyond the investment we make to be sure we can show up and gather with others for a worship service. There is a deeper cost when we decide to worship God. In worship we give the gift of concentrating sustained attention on God. We seek to authentically bring the fullness of our emotional life before God as we worship. We submit to follow the leading and prompting he gives through worship experience. Worship always costs something.

SIGNIFICANT SCRIPTURE

Isaiah 6:1 and 2 Chronicles 26

ILLUSTRATION | A Long-Term Leader

Uzziah reigned for a long time. If you do a study of the kings of Israel and Judah, you quickly discover that some of them had short runs as king. But Uzziah ruled in Jerusalem for fifty-two years. Try to get your mind around what it would feel like for an American to have a leader in office for fifty-two years.

To put this into context, think about how many men have held the office of president over the past fifty-two years. To illustrate this there is a Power Point slide that lists the following presidents:

- George W. Bush
- Bill Clinton
- George Bush Sr.
- Ronald Reagan
- Jimmy Carter
- Gerald Ford
- Richard Nixon
- Lyndon Johnson
- John F. Kennedy
- Dwight Eisenhower
- Harry Truman

Uzziah's reign spanned the time that all of these men served as president.

HISTORICAL CONTEXT | The Year Uzziah Died

Isaiah 6 begins with these words: "In the year that King Uzziah died." The prophet begins this way for some specific reasons. Uzziah became king of Israel when he was only sixteen years old. He was a remarkable leader. Many of his accomplishments are listed in 2 Chronicles 26.

Uzziah was a military genius. He built an army of more than 300,000 soldiers. The Bible says that he built machines designed by skillful men that could shoot arrows and sling large rocks. Under him, the Philistines were finally defeated. Other enemies, like the Ammonites, brought tribute to him.

He was a builder. He fortified the walls of Jerusalem. Under him, Jerusalem was finally safe. He was a technological innovator. He was an economic wizard. He developed a widespread system of cisterns for gathering water and developed Israel's agricultural economy.

Uzziah was also a spiritual leader. He was instructed and trained to follow God by a prophet named Zechariah (not the one who wrote the second to the last book of the Old Testament). The Bible says that he did what was right in the eyes of the Lord.

His fame spread as far as Egypt. With the possible exception of David and Solomon, he was remembered as the most powerful king Israel ever had.

LIFE APPLICATION | What Do You Do When Uzziah Dies?

Most of the people of Judah could only remember one leader ruling in Jerusalem. For their whole life, Uzziah had been on the throne. He was their anchor. He was a source of strength and confidence for the nation. He was their king.

Now Uzziah was dead. And Assyria, an emerging superpower, was gobbling up little nations like Judah. The people were getting nervous. If Uzziah was on the throne, he would know what to do. But the king was dead.

What do you do when Uzziah dies?

What do you do when your anchor breaks loose and you feel like you are cut afloat? How do you respond when the very thing you count on falls away? What do you do when:

- you lose your job?
- your tenacity wanes?
- your money runs out?
- your rock-solid relationship begins to shake?
- everything you were counting on begins to unravel and there's no more safety net?

This was the question being asked by the people of Judah in the days of Isaiah. What do you do when Uzziah dies?

Every follower of Jesus has to ask the question: What will I do when the things I place my trust in fall apart and let me down? Where will I look?

ON THE LIGHTER SIDE | Channel Surfing

Channel surfing is the exercise of sitting riveted to a TV set and going from channel to channel, often at a fairly rapid pace. Some people can spend a whole evening, a Saturday, or even an entire weekend surfing from channel to channel.

Invite those gathered to a moment of true confessions. Ask the following questions:

- How many of you have ever engaged in an activity known as channel surfing? (Invite people to raise their hands.)
- How many of you found out that channel surfing changed your life for the better?
- When was the last time you heard somebody say, "Last night I channel surfed all night long, from dinner until midnight, and I'm so glad I did. It was such a great experience. I feel like a new person today."

The truth of the matter is that most time spent channel surfing ends up being wasted time. It is the time we unplug our brains, put everything in neutral, and "veg out."

INTERPRETIVE INSIGHT | The King Is Dead . . . The King Lives!

Isaiah learned what to do when Uzziah dies. He turns his eyes from the temporary, earthly throne of a man to the eternal throne of God! Uzziah is dead, but God is alive. The throne of Judah is empty, but the throne of heaven is occupied. The king of Judah is gone, but God will never leave. Isaiah needs to remember what we all need to learn, that there is One seated on the throne of heaven and he reigns over the affairs of human beings.

2. The Confrontation: Seeing God

INTERPRETIVE INSIGHT | Heavenly Beings

As Isaiah sees the glory of the King of heaven, he also sees that God is surrounded by angelic beings. Isaiah tries to use words to communicate this spiritual reality. He points out that the seraphs used two wings to cover their faces. They are covering their faces because of the unspeakable holiness of God. We are told that no one can see God's face and live, and these beings seem to get the point. They are not fallen, but even they don't dare look directly on the glory of God.

Isaiah also points out that these heavenly beings are covering their feet with another set of wings. Back in those days, feet were a sign of earthliness. They were what connected people to the ground, so covering them was a sign of honor and respect. We see this in Exodus, when God revealed himself to Moses through the burning bush and said: "Take off your sandals, for the place where you are standing is holy ground" (Exodus 3:5).

SIGNIFICANT SCRIPTURE

Isaiah 6:2-3; Exodus 3:5; Matthew 5:8

HISTORICAL CONTEXT | Understanding the Hebrew

Isaiah sees these heavenly beings flying with wings covering their faces and feet. They are crying out, "Holy, holy, holy is the LORD Almighty." We may wonder why the angelic beings declare God's holiness three times. R. C. Sproul helps to clarify by pointing out that in English, we have many ways to emphasize something. If we want to get somebody's attention when we're writing, we can put the words in capital letters, italicize, or use an exclamation!

In the Hebrew language they did not have these options. In ancient Hebrew there were no vowels and little punctuation. There were also no lowercase letters. Hebrew was just a run of consonants with little dots (or else spaces) between words. In other words, the beginning of Isaiah 6 would have read:

N TH YR THT KNG WZZH DD

Or, since they read from right to left, it would have been:

DD HZZW GNK THT RY HT N

Isaiah 6:3, then, would look something like this (going left to right):

ND TH WR CLLNG T N NTHR
HL HL HL S TH LRD
LMGHT TH WHL RTH S
FLL F HS GLR

To help those gathered see the complexity of emphasizing something in Hebrew, you can use the slides provided in the Power Point presentation.

The main way in the Hebrew language to emphasize something was repetition, repetition, repetition. When the ancient scribes repeated something, it tended to stand out more. The repetition of the word "holy" stands out in Isaiah 6:3. This was the Hebrew way of adding emphasis.

NEW TESTAMENT CONNECTION

Who Will See God?

We begin to get a sense for the greatness of God's holiness when we see heavenly beings actually covering their faces in his presence. In light of this, we should be amazed at what Jesus says in the Sermon on the Mount. Jesus tells the people: "Blessed are the pure in heart, for they will see God" (Matthew 5:8).

What a staggering reality. Through Jesus Christ we can experience cleansing from sin and a new heart. Through Jesus our hearts are made so pure that we can be confident that one day we will see God face to face. We won't have to hide our face, wear a veil, or cover it with anything. We will see the holy God of heaven face to face because of the purity that is imparted to us through Jesus.

INTERPRETIVE INSIGHT

The Holiness of God

Sometimes in the Bible a word gets mentioned twice. This was only used when something was very important and needed emphasis. Jesus often would say, "Truly, truly." (The words he used in Greek were actually "Amen, amen.") It was his way of getting the attention of those who were listening, helping them realize that what he was about to say was of the utmost importance.

On a handful of occasions a word gets repeated three times in the Bible. This elevates it to a matter of ultimate importance. But only once in the Old Testament (Isaiah 6:3) and once in the New Testament (Revelation 4:8) is an attribute of God elevated to this level. It is interesting to note that God is never called, "Loving, loving, loving." He is never addressed as, "Just, just, just." Nowhere in all the Bible do we read, "Compassionate, compassionate, compassionate." Although God is absolutely loving, just, and compassionate, these attributes are never repeated three times. Only the holiness of God gets the x3 symbol next to it. Holiness gets to the core of who our God is.

LIFE APPLICATION

Setting Aside Distractions

True worship is always costly. It is the opposite of casual. It involves an investment of self. When we understand the nature of worship, we no longer make casual commitments. We don't say, "If I have time . . . ," "If it's convenient . . . ," "If I like the style . . . ," "When I can get around to it . . ." We don't worship God with a casual spirit. We don't drift in and out of attention as if we are channel surfing.

As we grow in worship, we no longer have an attitude that says, "If something tickles my fancy, then I'll pay attention." We don't worship with a casual attitude. We can't stomach the idea of singing songs about devotion and then go and live the same old self-centered way.

True worship means that we learn to do what the angels did. We come with our whole person before God. We carefully focus our thoughts and our emotions on him. We sing with all our heart, even when we don't really like the tune, because God deserves our undivided praise. We listen intently to the preached

ON THE LIGHTER SIDE

"Marcia, Marcia, Marcia!"

Even in English we sometimes use repetition to emphasize what we are saying. One very unsophisticated example can be found in a classic episode of *The Brady Bunch*. Jan, the middle sister in the family, is trying to communicate her frustration about how her older sister, Marcia, seems to get all the attention and that everything always seems to go Marcia's way. What does she say to express her heartfelt frustration?

"Marcia, Marcia, Marcia."

word even if the teaching style is not what we like, because we know that God wants to speak each time his Word is opened.

We set aside everything that could distract us, and we strain, with all our strength, to see the Lord seated on his throne. We do all we can to enter the presence of God, who is high and exalted. We stand in awe of his majestic glory, and we respond to him with our voices, bodies, hearts, lives, and all that is in us. When we commit to worship, we purpose in our hearts to take every possible distraction and set it aside because we are going to do the most important thing of all. We are going to worship the God who made us and loves us.

WORD STUDY

Qadosh

It is a challenge to define precisely what "holiness" is. Most people think of moral purity when they try to define holiness. That's an important part of it. But it is not at the core of how we should understand holiness.

The Hebrew word *qadosh* meant separate or set apart. It is something or someone that was wholly other. Imagine the most awe-inspiring moment in your life, where you were so amazed by what you saw, heard, or felt. Take that sense of wonder, mystery, and awe and multiply it by infinity. Only then can you begin to get a glimpse of the effect that God's holiness has on a human being. God is wholly other. There is nothing, no one, like him in all creation. God is an eternally self-sufficient, burning, transcendent, brilliant, perfect being. He is "Holy, holy, holy."

That is why the heavenly beings cry out, "The whole earth is full of his glory." The whole earth can no more contain all of God's glory than a thimble can contain Niagara Falls. This is the God, this holy God, we are called to worship.

3. The Conversion: Changed by God

ILLUSTRATION | "A Little Crease"

Isaiah saw himself as he was, and he spoke the truth about his own condition. This is rare indeed! More often, we look at ourselves and downplay our sin and weaknesses. We suffer from something called a self-serving bias. This occurs when we minimize the reality of our sin, the cost of our wrong choices, and the damage we have done to ourselves and others.

Imagine a teenage son who borrows his father's car for the first time. He has permission, and his father has given very detailed instructions on the use of this particular automobile. While pulling into a parking space, the teenage son catches the side of the car on a light post. When he gets out of the car and looks at the damage, he sees a long scrape in the paint and a crease in the body of the car. He calls his father and tries to explain what happened.

"I was being very careful. I didn't see the light post there. It's really just a little scrape and a small crease in the body of the car. I don't think it will cost much to fix it." When the teenage son gives this information, he really means it. It is dark out. He is not looking really closely. He hopes that it is no big deal. His own self-serving bias leads him to believe it is not a problem and that someone can probably pound the crease out with relative ease.

The next day, in broad daylight, the man at the body shop has a whole different understanding of the extent of the damage. He sees things the way they really are. He knows the real damage, and he knows the cost involved in repairing it. This is not going to be an easy pound-it-out deal. It will be a whole new part deal!

When Isaiah steps into the light of God's holiness, he says, "Woe to me! . . . I am ruined," because he sees the true condition of his soul. His self-serving bias is gone, and he realizes that only God can remake him.

We literally could not survive God's holiness. Emotionally, psychologically, we literally could not survive it.

DALLAS WILLARD

PAUSE FOR PRAYER

In the Presence of the Holy God

"Holy! Holy! Holy! You are the Lord God Almighty! You love us with a holy love. You forgive us with a holy mercy. We are filled with wonder and amazement at the eternal fellowship of the Trinity. We stand in awe of who you are—one God in three persons: Father, Son, and Holy Spirit. We thank you that you notice us, care for us, and love us with a passion that is beyond our comprehension. We honor you. We offer you our reverence as we lift our worship and praise. We do this all in Jesus' name, Amen."

NARRATIVE ON THE TEXT | "I Am Ruined!"

At the throne of God, Isaiah sees the full extent of his ruin and darkness. The sight almost destroys him. Apart from God's grace, Isaiah would be completely destroyed. He is undone when he sees himself in the light of God's holiness. Then, the angel takes a live coal from the altar and brings it to Isaiah. Isaiah stands there and allows it to touch his lips, one of the most sensitive parts of the human body.

Can you imagine what it would be like to have someone approach your mouth with a live coal? Do you think you'd just stand there? Through Isaiah we learn that there is real pain, a real sting, to the process of confession and repentance. Some people think that experiencing grace means they will never feel pain. Isaiah learned that deep grace can often mean feeling deep pain.

INTERPRETIVE INSIGHT | Redeemed Character

The goal of God's grace is *not* primarily to spare us from pain. It is to redeem our character. Experiencing remorse and sorrow over our sin is an important part of this process. If you were to ask a judge or parole board whether genuine remorse matters in their decision to let a criminal go free, they will tell you that it is extremely important.

ILLUSTRATION | When Words Cut like a Knife

On the CD of this message (found in OTC Kit 4), John Ortberg tells a story about a time that his words hurt another person very deeply. He also tells about the pain he felt when he realized how deeply he had wounded another person. You might want to tell a story from your own experience about a time you learned how dangerous our unclean lips can be.

CREATIVE MESSAGE IDEA | An Invitation to Worship

Consider stopping at this point in the message to spend some time in worship as a congregation. Invite those gathered to seek to be authentic before God during this time. Here are some ideas you can incorporate into worship:

Read: (These can be read in unison or by someone on your worship team.)

- Psalm 99
- Revelation 5:6–14
- Revelation 7:9–17

Sing

- "Holy, Holy, Holy," Reginald Heber / John Dykes
- "Holy, Holy," Jimmy Owens
- "Open the Eyes of My Heart," Paul Baloche
- "We All Bow Down," Lenny LeBlanc

Pray, celebrating the majesty and holiness of God

- If it would fit into your service, invite people to offer short prayers out loud (be sure to provide a microphone if needed).
- If it would fit into your style of worship, invite people to gather in clusters of three and four people and offer up short prayers.
- You may want to use the prayer supplied in this resource guide.

ILLUSTRATION | Hitting Bottom

Those who have walked through the pain of loving someone who battles alcoholism have heard the term "hitting bottom." This is when a person finally hits a place where he or she sees what alcoholism has done. They see the wasted years, the trashed relationships, the costly lies, the utter selfishness, and the low place they have ended up. In short, they see themselves as they really are.

In a spiritual sense, Isaiah has hit bottom. He sees himself as he really is, and he does not like what he sees. When Isaiah says, "Woe to me! . . . I am ruined," it is not a matter of neurotic, false guilt. It is the beginning of healing. It is his first step toward grace. When he hits bottom, he begins to look upward!

LIFE APPLICATION | A Desire to Be Clean

When we see ourselves as we really are, in the light of God's holiness, we become strongly motivated to be cleansed and made right. Like Isaiah, we are ready to pay whatever price we need to so that we might experience God's healing. Rather than running from the reality of our sinfulness, we are ready to confess it, acknowledge the pain we have caused God and others, and repent.

Christians used to speak of the gift of tears. They would even ask God to give them tears and a broken heart. They would seek the face of God and ask for his light to penetrate their souls and reveal the presence of sin. Their deep desire was that they would be led to a place of authentic repentance that led to cleansing.

Invite those gathered to enter a time of private confession and repentance. Ask God to show each person what they need to see in themselves. As people are in this time of quiet prayer and reflection, you might want to share a few prompting thoughts:

- Maybe there is an attitude of jealousy, judgment, or anger God wants to speak to you about.
- Maybe you are driven by the wrong things.
- Maybe there is something you did that has hurt another person and it needs to be set right.
- Maybe you battle with a mouth that lies, slanders, or gossips.
- Maybe you struggle with pride in your heart.
- Maybe God wants you to see that you have a heart that is cold and loveless.

Take a quiet time of confession and ask God for healing.

WORD STUDY
Woe

When Isaiah sees the living, holy God, his first response is not excitement. He does not celebrate that he's been singled out for something special. He doesn't start thinking about how he can impress other people with his amazing spiritual experience. He says, "Woe. . ." That's a very important, prophetic word. It was the word the prophets used to pronounce judgment. All through the Prophets, the word "woe" is a flag that indicates words of judgment will follow. Likewise, when Jesus spoke of God's judgment on the religious leaders of his day, he said, "Woe to you, teachers of the law and Pharisees, you hypocrites!" (Matthew 23:23, 25, 27, 29).

What is unique and unprecedented about Isaiah is that when he says "Woe," he is getting ready to pronounce judgment *on himself*. He says, "Woe to me! . . . I am ruined!" The prophets often said "Woe" as they spoke of God's judgment on nations, but Isaiah alone declares a "Woe" on himself. When Isaiah sees the holiness of God, it causes him to see the full extent of the darkness in his own being. He is shattered. The true condition of the depths of his soul—his real thoughts, motives, desires, petty cruelty, and the unrelenting selfishness—becomes visible to him for the first time, and he is horrified. Only one word makes sense at a moment like that: "Woe!"

SIGNIFICANT SCRIPTURE

Isaiah 6:8-9; 49:6; Acts 8:26-39

PAUSE FOR PRAYER

Ask God to tear down division in your city and to build unity among all people. Ask God to build strong churches in every neighborhood. Pray for unity among churches that serve Jesus. Ask God to help each person gathered to offer their life to him in a new way saying, "Here I am, Lord, send me!"

4. The Call: Led by God

INTERPRETIVE INSIGHT | Moving into Action

God doesn't cleanse Isaiah just for his own sake. God has a calling for him. He says, "Whom shall I send? And who will go for us?" Of course, God is not perplexed about this. He asks the question so that Isaiah can freely choose to go.

Isaiah says, "Here am I. Send me!" Spiritually authentic worship always ends with a heart that is willing to follow God. Worship is never just about having an intense emotional experience. It's never simply about how I feel when I am done. Authentic worship always costs something. It costs us a submitted life.

NEW TESTAMENT CONNECTION | A New Day

In Acts 8:26-39 we read about Philip's encounter with an Ethiopian eunuch. This man was excluded from Israel on multiple levels, but again we see God's arms wide open. Here we see that everyone is welcome, if they will only come through faith in Jesus.

In this story Philip was led by the Holy Spirit to encounter a man who was a foreigner and a eunuch. God tells Philip, "I want this man included in my people."

Here is a bonus question: When Philip met this man, he was reading from a book in the Old Testament. Which one was it? Right! It was Isaiah!

After a conversation and a time of teaching, the Holy Spirit inspired Philip to offer baptism to this man. In that moment, through faith in Jesus, this foreign eunuch became part of God's family.

Jesus also addressed this issue of the open arms of the Father. He said: "My house will be called a house of prayer for all nations" (Mark 11:17).

NEW TESTAMENT CONNECTION | Time to Mourn

For true repentance to take place, we must set aside denial, rationalization, and excuses. We must reflect on what we have done from the perspective of those we have hurt. We must be willing to see ourselves as we truly are and allow our hearts to be broken when we see the depth and costliness of our sin. This is why James says:

Come near to God and he will come near to you. Wash your hands, you sinners, and purify your hearts, you double-minded. Grieve, mourn and wail. Change your laughter to mourning and your joy to gloom. Humble yourselves before the Lord, and he will lift you up. (James 4:8-10)

Notice the verbs in the middle of that text—*grieve, mourn and wail*. This is a command. James is not talking about wallowing in neurotic guilt. He is talking about entering deeply into God's sorrow over sin.

LIFE APPLICATION | Radical Reconciliation

Close with a challenge for those gathered to seek healing and restoration wherever there are broken relationships. If your church has ministries that are seeking God's reconciliation with those who have been outsiders, highlight these ministries and encourage involvement.

My soul is like a mirror in which the glory of God is reflected, but sin, however insignificant, covers the mirror with smoke.
SAINT THERESA

HISTORICAL CONTEXT | Who Is Welcome?

Later in the book of Isaiah we get more insight into the call of Isaiah. We read these words spoken by God:

It is too small a thing for you to be my
servant
to restore the tribes of Jacob
and bring back those of Israel I have
kept.
I will also make you a light for the
Gentiles,
that you may bring my salvation
to the ends of the earth.
(Isaiah 49:6)

This idea of God being a light for all the Gentiles is radical and new. Up to this point, God's people considered those who belonged to the nations as excluded from God's love and plan. Foreigners were not thought to be welcome, eunuchs were excluded, and many others were not invited. But now, everything is going to change. Everyone will be welcome!

CREATIVE MESSAGE IDEA | Confession and Forgiveness

Songs

- "Just as I Am," Charlotte Elliott / William Bradbury
- "Whiter than Snow," James Nicholson / William Fischer
- "Create in Me a Clean Heart," Norman Johnson

Scriptures

- Isaiah 6:7
- Psalm 51
- Psalm 103:8-12
- 1 John 1:8-9

Prayer

Pray for each person to experience the freedom that comes with forgiveness for all who confess their sins through Jesus Christ. Ask the Holy Spirit to grant the power needed to resist sin and walk in holiness.

Sharing

When we confess and repent, we don't stop there. We need to hear God's promise of forgiveness. Since we are a priesthood of believers (1 Peter 2:9), we can remind each other of the truth that true confession always leads to forgiveness and a new beginning.

Invite those gathered to turn to someone and say something like, "Through Jesus, your sins are forgiven."

SESSION 5

Hezekiah: Radical Trust

2 KINGS 16:7–8; ISAIAH 7:1–8:18; 36:1–37:38

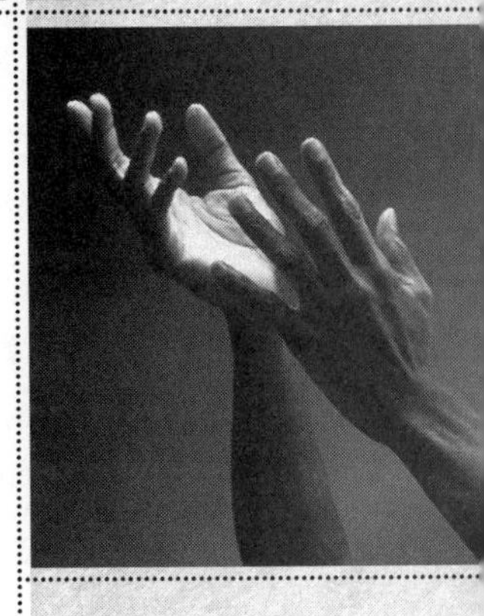

The Heart of the **MESSAGE**

The history of the Old Testament records the stories of two radically different kings of Judah. Ahaz is an example of a life driven by fear. Rather than placing his trust in God, he trusts in the military might and political alliances. In contrast, King Hezekiah stands as an example of radical trust in God. Rather than take the easy route of establishing strategic military and political alliances, he looks to God as his source of strength.

God invites us into a relationship based on trust. Though we live in a world that can cause great fear and anxiety, God offers another path. Radical trust is God's plan for all followers of Jesus. Through the example of Ahaz we learn of the folly of fear, and through the life of Hezekiah, the pathway of trust.

The Heart of the **MESSENGER**

Many devoted followers of Jesus face ongoing battles with fear and anxiety, but it really is possible to live with a deep level of trust in God. The apostle Paul gives this exhortation:

> Do not be anxious about anything, but in everything, by prayer and petition, with thanksgiving, present your requests to God. And the peace of God, which transcends all understanding, will guard your hearts and your minds in Christ Jesus. (Philippians 4:6–7)

As you prepare to bring this message, take time to examine your heart and life. Are there places where anxiety and fear have control? Maybe you have faced a conflict with someone in your church and it is causing you to worry. Possibly your ministry is facing financial pressures and you are dealing with anxiety over this. Lay any area of anxiety you are facing before God in prayer and ask him to help you learn to walk in deeper levels of trust.

Brief Message **OUTLINE**

1. Understanding the Times
2. The Example of Ahaz: Fear and Folding
3. The Example of Hezekiah: Radical Trust

1. Understanding the Times

NARRATIVE ON THE TEXT | Empire-Building

As we read the Old Testament, it becomes apparent that the nations all around Canaan had a hard time getting along with each other. They were all trying to build their own empire. In most cases the process of empire-building was not about national honor; rather, it was about economic prosperity and survival.

All nations have to face the reality of debt and economic problems at some point in their history. In those days the kings wanted to build palaces, roads, and other national projects. They also had to maintain a military for the protection of their cities. There was no banking system, no loans to be negotiated for all they had to do. Thus, the kings of these nations would invade and take over a neighboring country. This was instant income! At the same time, they would take some of the best people of the country and force them to be slaves for their projects.

In addition, invasion provided an ongoing source of revenue for years to come. Once they ruled a nation, they forced them to pay annual tribute. The process of empire-building and expansion was motivated by the need for wealth more than anything else.

HISTORICAL CONTEXT | Map Time

God calls Abraham out of *Mesopotamia.* God says to him, "Leave your country, your people and your father's household and go to the land I will show you" (Genesis 12:1).

Abraham's response is staggering. He simply packs up his family and possessions and heads out. They travel to the region of *Canaan.* Abraham and his descendants—Isaac, Jacob, and Joseph—live in Canaan until a famine drives them to *Egypt.*

While in Egypt the Israelites multiply rapidly. They become Pharaoh's slaves and his source of manpower for many of his massive building projects. God later calls Moses to lead the people out of Egypt. They end up taking the long way on their journey from Egypt to the Promised Land. They spend forty years in the *Sinai Desert.* Then, they enter the *Promised Land of Canaan* and become a nation.

Once the nation is settled in the land and after the time of the Judges, Israel has a succession of kings: Saul, then David, and then Solomon. These three leaders rule over the united kingdom. After Solomon, the nation is split into two countries through a time of civil war.

When the dust settles, there are two nations rather than one. The *northern kingdom,* commonly called Israel, is made up of ten tribes; their capital is Samaria. Jeroboam is their king. The *southern kingdom,* most often called Judah, is made up of two tribes; they have their capital in Jerusalem, with Rehoboam as their ruler.

These two nations are surrounded by many other small countries who are their enemies. Over on the coast are the *Philistines.* Down to the south is *Edom.* Over to the east is *Moab.* A little further north is *Ammon.* These are, in many cases, barbaric, backward, primitive people. To understand what is happening during the reign of the kings of Judah the geography is important.

2. The Example of Ahaz: Fear and Folding

NARRATIVE ON THE TEXT | Where Will You Turn?

SIGNIFICANT SCRIPTURE

Isaiah 7:1-25

In Isaiah 7 we read that Assyria is on the march. The Assyrians are in a process of empire-building and are swallowing up small countries all around Canaan. These small countries realize that they are vulnerable, so some of them begin to look for possible military alliances. Israel (the northern kingdom) and Aram form an alliance. They decide to join forces to try to resist the Assyrian army. They come to Ahaz king of Judah and invite him to join their alliance.

For the sake of self-preservation, it seems like Ahaz would say yes. But Ahaz says, "No." He wants nothing to do with a battle against Assyria.

Thus, the kings of Israel and Aram decide to go to war against Ahaz (and Judah). Their hope is to conquer Judah and force them to stand with them against the imminent Assyrian invasion. When Ahaz hears that Israel and Aram have formed an alliance and are coming against his nation, we read these words: "The hearts of Ahaz and his people were shaken, as the trees of the forest are shaken by the wind" (Isaiah 7:2).

What a vivid picture! Ahaz and the people of Judah feel trapped. Not only is Assyria on the march, but Israel and Aram are plotting against them. The people of Judah are trembling like trees of the forest when the winds blow! They are shaking in their boots. Isaiah paints a colorful picture of the anxiety and fear that has gripped the heart of Ahaz and Judah.

HISTORICAL CONTEXT | The Rise of Assyria

One of the reasons Israel was able to exist as a nation for many centuries was that there were no dominant superpowers in their region for much of their history. There were superpowers in the ancient world, such as Egypt, Babylonia, Assyria, and Persia. But for several centuries, all of them were dormant. Then, around 700 B.C. Assyria began its ascendancy. It started taking over smaller countries all around Israel. As the army took over a country, they sought to leave behind the smallest occupational force possible. The goal was to retain control of the region but not weaken their own military force by spreading them out too thinly. They wanted the core of their army to be able to fight new battles and conquer other countries.

What Assyria (and other ancient nations) learned was that if they conquered a country and left a small force occupying the land, with time the people would revolt. As a result, they started sending thousands of people into exile and replacing them with people from other nations. When this was done, it took a much smaller occupational army to maintain control of a region because the people had lost their sense of national identity. This is exactly what happened to Israel (the northern kingdom) in 712 B.C.

The question of the hour becomes, *Where will Ahaz and Judah turn in this desperate hour?* They don't want to throw their lot in with Israel and Aram. They know Assyria is too powerful for them to handle. Where will they turn?

Isaiah knows what temptation will face Ahaz—that Ahaz is contemplating an unthinkable option. Ahaz is considering an alliance with Assyria. Since the Assyrians are the rising superpower, an alliance with them will grant Judah protection from invasion and a guarantee that Israel and Aram will back off!

INTERPRETIVE INSIGHT | The Company You Keep

To Ahaz, forming an alliance seems like a good idea. But this was not God's plan for the nation of Judah. God is about to use Assyria to bring judgment on the northern kingdom—on Israel—because of their unfaithfulness and their treatment of the poor. But Assyria will also be coming under judgment because of their idolatry, corruption, violence, and paganism. God does not want Judah in partnership with *either* of these nations. Their company is bad company! To partner with them is to enter into their rebellion and sin. It also means taking the possible risk of coming under God's judgment of them.

What God wants is for his people to place their trust in him. Rather than running to the new superpower or bowing to the pressure of neighboring nations, God longs for his people to place their trust in his ability to save them.

NARRATIVE ON THE TEXT | Ask for a Sign

God knows that Ahaz is fearful and weak. Thus, he sends Isaiah to bring a word of encouragement:

> "Say to him, 'Be careful, keep calm and don't be afraid. Do not lose heart because of these two smoldering stubs of firewood—because of the fierce anger of Rezin and Aram and of the son of Remaliah. Aram, Ephraim and Remaliah's son have plotted your ruin, saying, "Let us invade Judah; let us tear it apart and divide

NEW TESTAMENT CONNECTION

The Samaritans

After the northern kingdom was defeated, Israel ceased to exist as a distinct nation. But, many Israelites were still living in the land along with many imported non-Israelites. Since Samaria had been the capital of Israel, these people were later called the Samaritans. They were a mixture of Israelite blood but also foreign blood. These people had the books of Moses from the Old Testament, but they did not have the prophetic books. They were syncretistic in their religious beliefs and worshiped the God of Israel, but also other gods.

That's why the Samaritans were shunned by the Jewish people in Jesus' day. They were seen as half-Jews at best, and enemies at worst. This is why, in the gospel of John, we read about the kind of tension that existed between Jews and Samaritans. Jesus once engaged a Samaritan woman in conversation, and she is shocked. In John 4:9 we read: "The Samaritan woman said to him, 'You are a Jew and I am a Samaritan woman. How can you ask me for a drink?' (For Jews do not associate with Samaritans.)"

HISTORICAL CONTEXT | Sources of National Income: Taxes, Tolls, and Tribute

There were three primary ways an empire would gain wealth in the Old Testament times. The first way was by *taxing their own people*. This was a common practice. It is fair to say that taxes were as popular then as they are now. A second source of revenue for a nation was *road tolls*. They charged people to use their roads and travel through their territory. Third, wealth was increased by forcing a conquered nation to pay *tribute*. The conquered nation was looted of much of its treasures and then required to pay an annual tribute to their rulers.

it among ourselves, and make the son of Tabeel king over it." Yet
this is what the Sovereign LORD says:

> "'It will not take place,
> it will not happen.'" (Isaiah 7:4–7)

God wants Ahaz to take heart. The two kings who are threatening him are like smoldering stubs of firewood. They can make all the threats they want, but God says that their words are idle threats. Their bark is bigger than their bite. No matter what they may threaten, God says it will not happen.

Then, God speaks these words to Ahaz:

> If you do not stand firm in your faith,
> you will not stand at all. (Isaiah 7:9)

God is speaking to Ahaz and doing everything possible to strengthen and fortify him. First, God assures Ahaz that Israel will not conquer Judah. Second, God calls him to stand strong in faith. Then, in a shocking manner, God invites Ahaz to ask for a sign. This is unusual in the Old Testament. But because Ahaz has such weak faith, God offers to give him a sign. This is not meant to be a normative practice. It is a concession God offers because Ahaz is faltering.

ON THE LIGHTER SIDE

Thank Heaven for 7-11

Listen to the words of Isaiah 7:11: "Ask the LORD your God for a sign, whether in the deepest depths or in the highest heights."

You can almost hear Ahaz saying, "Thank heaven for 7-11!"

ON THE LIGHTER SIDE

Tolls Are No Fun

In some parts of the United States and other places in the world there are toll roads. Nobody really likes to stop and pay tolls, but it is a reality that many people live with on a daily basis. In recent years many of these toll roads have tried to speed things up by developing a technology where a person can buy a pass that pays for many tolls. These people don't have to stop and toss in a handful of change; they drive right through a special lane and a scanner deducts the toll from their pass. It is a real time saver!

In the Chicago area there are many toll roads. A gentleman had borrowed a friend's BMW and was using it as he drove on the toll roads. This car was set up so that it could drive right through the hi-speed lane and not have to stop. His first time through the toll area he slowed down to about five miles per hour to make sure he heard the beep and knew the toll was paid. The second time he came to a toll area he went through the special lane at fifteen miles an hour, and it beeped again.

So, the third time he came to a toll area, he was pretty confident that the technology was working. Everyone else had to slow down and toss their change in the machine, or worse, stop and hand money over to an attendant. He cruised through at fifty miles an hour. The only problem was that this time he forgot to go through the special passing lane. He went right through one of the regular tollbooth lanes at fifty miles an hour and the wooden arm was down. He hit the arm and it exploded. It shook him up so bad that he drove for several miles before he could make himself stop the car.

INTERPRETIVE INSIGHT | Keeping Your Options Open

We might think that Ahaz would be thrilled with the offer of a sign from God. It seems as if he would love some kind of sign to buttress his faith and guarantee that the nation of Judah would be safe. But his response is surprising and strange. Ahaz says: "I will not ask; I will not put the LORD to the test" (Isaiah 7:12).

At first glance it may seem as if Ahaz is being reverent by refusing a sign, as if he is doing the honorable thing. But this is not the case. Ahaz is covering his real intentions with a thin veneer of piety and spirituality. The real reason Ahaz won't ask God for a sign is that he wants to keep his options open. He wants to be able to jump in and follow God, or else to go the other way and disobey God if that seems like the better option.

Ahaz knows if he asks for a sign, God will give it and then his options will be limited. If he enters a conversation with God and agrees to submit to him, he will slam the door on the Assyrian option. In other words, when Ahaz says he does not want a sign, he is saying that he wants to keep his options open more than he wants to obey God.

NEW TESTAMENT CONNECTION

Immanuel

Although Ahaz may have been driven by wrong motives, God did give a sign. In the gospel of Matthew we read: "All this took place to fulfill what the Lord had said through the prophet: 'The virgin will be with child and will give birth to a son, and they will call him Immanuel'—which means, 'God with us.'" The final sign that God gives to fulfill this prophecy is Jesus, God with us.

NARRATIVE ON LIFE | The Truth about Human Nature

Ahaz reveals something that is deeply rooted in human nature. We like to do what is right, but we also want to keep our options open. We often try to keep an escape route, even though we may know God will not approve of it. We would like to be honest, but if we find ourselves in a desperate situation, we are ready to lie if we have to.

God wants to reveal his presence and power and invite us into a life of full devotion. We tend to prefer convenient and limited levels of devotion that allow us to keep a few options on the back burner just in case.

ON THE LIGHTER SIDE | A Sunday School Lesson

There's an old story about a girl in a Sunday school class who got her Bible verses a little bit mixed up. One Sunday morning her teacher asked the class to explain what a lie is. She said, "A lie is an abomination under the Lord and a very present help in time of trouble."

Sadly there are a lot of people who live as if they are confident that verse must be in the Bible somewhere. They say, "I'd like to tell the truth. I'd like to put away deceit, falsehood, hype, and spinning. But if push comes to shove, a little lie can be a very present help in a time of need."

LIFE APPLICATION | Limiting Our Options

It's scary to say, "I'm going to cut myself off from my sinful options. I'm only going to speak truth. I'm not going to spin or manipulate or hype anyone." Such an intentional limiting of options will be new territory for many people. Too many followers of Christ practice exactly what Ahaz does. Because of fear and anxiety, we leave our options open and we dishonor God in the process.

Isaiah goes to incredible lengths to help Ahaz turn from fear and to learn how to trust in God. Ahaz has every opportunity to limit his options and surrender to God's will. In the same way, God invites us to willingly limit our options. Taking this step can look very different for each person who is seeking to be fully devoted to God.

NARRATIVE ON THE TEXT | What's in a Name?

God speaks to Isaiah, his prophet and says:

> "Take a large scroll and write on it with an ordinary pen: Maher-Shalal-Hash-Baz. And I will call in Uriah the priest and Zechariah son of Jeberekiah as reliable witnesses for me."
>
> Then I went to the prophetess, and she conceived and gave birth to a son. And the LORD said to me, "Name him Maher-Shalal-Hash-Baz. Before the boy knows how to say 'My father' or 'My mother,' the wealth of Damascus and the plunder of Samaria will be carried off by the king of Assyria." (Isaiah 8:1–4)

We discover that Isaiah is married and that both he and his wife are prophets. God is saying that Aram and Israel are about to be plundered by Assyria. Before the child (named Maher-Shalal-Hash-Baz) knows how to say the most basic words, "My father," or "My mother," Assyria is going to swallow up the two nations who have been threatening Judah and Ahaz.

The name Maher-Shalal-Hash-Baz has deep significance. It means "quick to the plunder." The name of this child points to the ruin that will be coming on Israel and Aram in a short time.

SIGNIFICANT SCRIPTURE

Isaiah 8:1-18 and 2 Kings 16:7-8

ON THE LIGHTER SIDE

A Mouthful

Aren't you glad you were not one of Isaiah's children? Wouldn't you hate going around with the name Maher-Shalal-Hash-Baz? You wouldn't just take a spelling test. You'd be the spelling test!

INTERPRETIVE INSIGHT | The Cost of Compromise

God assures Ahaz that Judah will be safe. He does all he can to calm the fears that drive Ahaz. Sadly, Ahaz will not trust God. He will not hear the warnings of the prophet. He will not trust the promise that Judah will be safe from any invasion of Israel and Aram. Ahaz goes on to make a deal with Assyria. He gets into bed with a nation that is far from God. He sells his soul because he is driven by fear. This decision ends up ruining his life.

In 2 Kings 16:7–8 we read:

> Ahaz sent messengers to say to Tiglath-Pileser king of Assyria, "I am your servant and vassal. Come up and save me out of the hand of the king of Aram and of the king of Israel, who are attacking me." And Ahaz took the silver and gold found in the temple of the LORD and in the treasuries of the royal palace and sent it as a gift to the king of Assyria.

Ahaz willingly becomes a puppet on the strings of the king of Assyria. He figures that in the political climate of his day, he will have to put his trust in somebody, so he goes with the biggest kid on the block, Assyria. He even takes the silver and gold that the people have given for the temple of God and sends it to the pagan ruler of Assyria.

Ahaz begins on a long slide deeper and deeper into sin. By the end of his life he has altars in Israel built to Assyrian gods. He leads the Israelites into idolatry. He places the body of his son in a fire and watches him burn to death as a sacrifice to pagan gods. When it was all said and done, Ahaz compromises in ways that cost him more than he ever dreamed.

Do you think Ahaz planned for his life to end up like this? Do you think he set out to murder his child, sacrifice his freedom, mislead his people, and betray his God? No one plans to shipwreck his or her life. But for Ahaz, and for many of us, fear can be a deciding factor. Fear leads Ahaz to begin a process of compromise that costs him pain and loss beyond description.

NEW TESTAMENT CONNECTION

No Fear

Certainly there is healthy fear and reverence of God. Proverbs teaches us that the fear of the Lord is the starting place of true wisdom. However, the kind of fear that paralyzes us, drives us from God, and causes us to compromise is never honoring to God. John writes and reminds us that we do not have to live in fear:

> In this way, love is made complete among us so that we will have confidence on the day of judgment, because in this world we are like him. There is no fear in love. But perfect love drives out fear, because fear has to do with punishment. The one who fears is not made perfect in love. (1 John 4:17–18)

NARRATIVE ON LIFE | The Fear Factor

Fear makes people selfish, impulsive, foolish, untrusting, and desperate. It dries up our ability for compassion and honesty. Once a human being is afraid, we never know what they can do. Sometimes we hear a voice inside our head that says, "You can't handle this. Even with God's help you will never be strong enough to make it." When we hear a voice speaking in our heart or head that says things like this, we can be confident it is not from God.

The Bible never says, "God panicked." In the entire Bible you will never read, "And then God said, 'What will I do now?'" God never panics and he never leads his people into panic. Ahaz leads a fear-based life, and it ends in disaster. Thankfully, we don't have to live like this. There is a better way.

3. The Example of Hezekiah: Radical Trust

SIGNIFICANT SCRIPTURE

Isaiah 36 and 37

NARRATIVE ON THE TEXT | A View from the Wall

The king of Assyria sends officials to intimidate the people and leaders of Judah. The field commander of Assyria enters a conversation with Hezekiah's officials in front of the walls of Jerusalem. All the people of Jerusalem are on the wall, listening to find out what's going to happen. They know that their king is standing in defiance of the king of Assyria. They know that Assyria is on the march.

The general of Assyria speaks to the leaders of Judah. He asks, "On what are you basing this confidence of yours?" He cannot imagine why Judah is willing to stand up against Assyrian might. He assumes that Hezekiah must be looking to Egypt to rescue them. But he is not.

Then this leader from Assyria takes a real shot at Hezekiah and Israel:

> "And if you say to me, 'We are depending on the LORD our God'—isn't he the one whose high places and altars Hezekiah removed, saying to Judah and Jerusalem, 'You must worship before this altar'?" (Isaiah 36:7)

The field commander from Assyria is taunting the people of Israel. He is questioning whether God is even on their side. He is seeking to undermine Hezekiah's spiritual leadership of the nation.

HISTORICAL CONTEXT | A New Time and a New King

In Isaiah 36 we meet a new king of Judah and discover another way to live. This story takes place several decades after Ahaz was king of Judah. The northern kingdom—Israel—no longer existed, since Assyria swallowed it up in 712 B.C. But one thing remains the same. There is political turmoil and the same superpower, Assyria, is threatening to conquer Judah.

The nation of Judah is standing strong, and much of their resolve comes from the courage of their king, a man named Hezekiah. The current king of Assyria, Sennacherib, is prepared to squash Judah like a bug. But he prefers to have Judah surrender so he wouldn't have to lose any soldiers. The time of Hezekiah is much like that of Ahaz, but he responds in a very different way.

INTERPRETIVE INSIGHT | Quality Control

The leader of Assyria's army has it all wrong. He has heard that Hezekiah has torn down altars and destroyed places of worship. He assumes this is a bad thing and that Hezekiah has angered the God of Judah. What he does not know is that Hezekiah has torn down *pagan* altars. He is seeking to drive the people back to the heart of God. It is a kind of quality control. Rather than have the people scattered all over the land worshiping at pagan altars, he wants them to come back to Jerusalem again. His actions are not offensive to God; rather, they honor God.

NARRATIVE ON THE TEXT | An Issue of Language

Next, the commander of Assyria's army shouts out words that would have sent shivers down the spines of all the people on the wall: "Furthermore, have I come to attack and destroy this land without the LORD? The LORD himself told me to march against this country and destroy it" (Isaiah 36:10).

This is too much for the leaders of Judah to take. Hezekiah's officials ask the leader of Assyria's army to speak in Aramaic, not in Hebrew: "Please speak to your servants in Aramaic, since we understand it. Don't speak to us in Hebrew in the hearing of the people on the wall" (Isaiah 36:11).

What they are actually saying is, "Let's make these negotiations private." In those days, Aramaic was the language of diplomacy. Many of the people would

HISTORICAL CONTEXT | Ancient Covenants

One of the exciting archaeological discoveries of the last century has been the unearthing of many ancient treaties (covenants) from the Hittite people. These covenants had certain elements that were uniform and very important. They were featured in all covenants back in those days. These elements were:

- *The preamble:* This portion identified the powerful king initiating the covenant and the people who would become his subjects or vassals through the covenant.
- *The historical review:* In this portion the more powerful king listed the many things he had done for the people.
- *Stipulations of the covenant:* These were statements about specific behavior that was expected by each of the two parties in the covenant.
- *Provisions for storage:* In the covenant agreement there were a number of copies of the covenant. This was important so they could be kept and read publicly.
- *Blessings and curses:* Next, associated with the covenant was a list of blessings you could expect if you kept up the covenant and a list of curses for those who broke the covenant.
- *Vow of faithfulness:* This is where people said, "I will be a covenant keeper."

In Exodus, and scattered throughout the whole rest of the Pentateuch, we find every one of these features. God is all about covenant.

What we have to keep in the forefront of our minds is that the laws were never intended to be a list of rules that somebody had to keep to earn salvation. These laws were given after God had redeemed his people from Egypt and called them his beloved children. They were intended to describe *what a covenant relationship with God was supposed to look like.* What would it look like to be a kingdom of priests and a holy nation?

have understood Hebrew but not Aramaic. The leaders of Judah are asking the commander of Assyria to stop trying to humiliate the king in front of his people.

The response of the Assyrian commander is emphatic: "Was it only to your master and you that my master sent me to say these things, and not to the men sitting on the wall—who, like you, will have to eat their own filth and drink their own urine?" (Isaiah 36:12). The field commander wants the people to know, in their own language, what lies ahead if they try to defy the king and army of Assyria. The comment about eating their own filth and drinking their own urine is not meant to be some kind of disgusting word picture. It is a threat of siege.

INTERPRETIVE INSIGHT | The Power of Fear

It is called psychological warfare! The commander of Assyria is intentionally speaking to all the people on the wall. He wants the word spread through Jerusalem. He knows that in a matter of hours rumors will be spreading all over the city. Rumors such as, "Hezekiah is deceiving us; God can't get us out of this situation." "We will all die of starvation when Assyria lays siege to the city." "There is no way we can resist the army of Assyria; we are as good as defeated already." That is what the commander of Assyria wants—it is what he expects!

HISTORICAL CONTEXT | The Threat of a Siege

In those days, one form of warfare was to surround a city and simply wait until the people were starving to death. At some point, when the conditions became bad enough, the people in the city would surrender. Throughout ancient history the people trapped in a city during a siege were driven to a point of desperation where they even considered cannibalism to stay alive. The commander of the Assyrian army is telling the people, "You had better hear what I say because you will come to a place of utter starvation if you refuse to obey the king of Assyria."

The Assyrians know that once the people are gripped by fear, their faith, loyalty, and unity will be gone. They know that fear will destroy confidence, paralyze the people, and turn them against each other. What was true about the power of fear is still true today.

Fear is the great enemy of spiritual community. Every time we choose fear over self-disclosure or being known, we paralyze community. Each time we choose fear over a needed confrontation, we weaken the fabric of Christian community. Every time we bow to fear and refuse to speak the truth in love, community dies a little.

NARRATIVE ON LIFE | Standing Firm

Building a healthy community does require boldness and fearlessness. In Isaiah 37, the prophet comes to Hezekiah to encourage him to respond in a God-honoring way to the threats he is facing. Isaiah has seen kings come and go. He saw Ahaz give in to fear and live with staggering consequences. But he tells Hezekiah the same thing he told Ahaz. "Trust God. Be brave. Stand in your faith."

The good news is, Hezekiah listens and follows the wise counsel of Isaiah. He doesn't surrender to Assyria. He stands firm in his faith. No matter what the odds, threats, or possible repercussions, Hezekiah commits to follow God and not human inclinations.

NARRATIVE ON THE TEXT | You Don't Have a Chance

Word of Hezekiah's bold refusal to bow to the might of Assyria gets back to the king of Assyria, Sennacherib. He hears that Judah is defying him and Hezekiah is trusting in God rather than him. We can be confident that Sennacherib, king of Assyria, is outraged!

He sits down and writes Hezekiah a letter. We need to remember that there were no telegrams or emails in those days. When communication happened, it could take days or weeks. Hezekiah, and the people of Israel, have undoubtedly been waiting to hear how Sennacherib will respond to Hezekiah's defiance.

They wait, and wait, and wait some more. And then, all of a sudden, Hezekiah gets a letter signed by the king of Assyria:

> "Say to Hezekiah king of Judah: Do not let the god you depend on deceive you when he says, 'Jerusalem will not be handed over to the king of Assyria.' Surely you have heard what the kings of Assyria have done to all the countries, destroying them completely. And will you be delivered? Did the gods of the nations that were destroyed by my forefathers deliver them. . . ?" (Isaiah 37:10–12)

The king of Assyria then runs through a laundry list of other countries defeated by his army. This is the worst news possible for Judah and Hezekiah. Sennacherib is saying, "I will completely destroy you and your puny little nation. I've done it before. I will do it again."

Humanly speaking, Sennacherib is absolutely right. The battle between Judah and the might of Assyria is no contest.

INTERPRETIVE INSIGHT | When the Pressure Is On . . . Pray!

What do you do when you get a letter from the most powerful and bloodthirsty ruler in the world and he wants you to know that he will be dropping in for a personal visit? How do you respond when you get the worst news of your life? Where do you turn when fear comes pounding on your front door?

The example of Hezekiah at this moment stands as a beacon for all who want to learn how to follow God. In Isaiah 37:15–20 we read:

> And Hezekiah prayed to the LORD: "O LORD Almighty, God of Israel, enthroned between the cherubim, you alone are God over all the kingdoms of the earth. You have made heaven and earth. Give ear, O LORD, and hear; open your eyes, O LORD, and see; listen to all the words Sennacherib has sent to insult the living God.
>
> "It is true, O LORD, that the Assyrian kings have laid waste all these peoples and their lands. They have thrown their gods into the fire and destroyed them, for they were not gods but only wood and stone, fashioned by human hands. Now, O LORD our God, deliver us from his hand, so that all kingdoms on earth may know that you alone, O LORD, are God."

Prayer is not overcoming God's reluctance; it is laying hold of His highest willingness.
RICHARD CHENEVIX TRENCH

Hezekiah goes to the one place where answers are found, courage is gathered, and hope is restored. He goes to prayer—the throne of God!

ON THE LIGHTER SIDE | Bambi Versus Godzilla

Back in the late 1960s a very short film named "Bambi Meets Godzilla" came out. It opened up with some credits and then a little deer grazing in a field. Then this giant foot came down and squashed Bambi. That was the end of the movie. Then the credits rolled. In the mind of Assyria and Judah, their battle would be a lot like "Bambi Meets Godzilla."

If you can find a copy of this short film, you might even want to show it.

LIFE APPLICATION | What Do You Need to Bring to God?

Hezekiah takes the letter from Sennacherib and spreads it out before the Lord. He seeks the face of God in prayer, and God hears him. In response, Isaiah sends a message from God to Hezekiah. He assures him that his prayers have been heard and that the threats of Sennacherib will not come to pass.

Here is the question each person must to ask: *What do I need to spread out before the Lord?*

Each of us gets letters from Assyria. A letter from Sennacherib can take many forms. It is anything that tempts us to be driven by fear. It is a piece of bad news that makes us so anxious we can't live for God. It is a threat from a person that robs us of a sense of trust and confidence that God can deliver. It is anything that unleashes fear in our lives:

- Maybe it's a piece of paper from work that says your services are no longer required.
- Maybe it's an assignment that seems too hard, or a performance review that has you worried, or an expectation that you're not sure you can fulfill.
- Maybe it's a test at school.
- Maybe it's a note from your bank with bad news.
- Maybe it's a bill you don't think you can pay.
- Maybe it's a looming black cloud of financial concerns.
- Maybe it's a word from a doctor or a diagnosis that's real bad.
- Maybe it's a letter from a teacher about one of your children.
- Maybe it's a word of rejection from someone you love.
- Maybe it's an email that cut you deeply.
- Maybe it's a painful letter from a lawyer's office.
- Maybe it's a deep-rooted anxiety that rules your heart.

Prayer is the key that unlocks all the storehouses of God's infinite grace and power. All that God is, and all that God has, is at the disposal of prayer.
R. A. TORRY

Hezekiah takes the worst letter with the worst news he's ever gotten in his life and spreads it out before the Lord. In response, God hears and answers. Like Hezekiah, we can bring our fear-producing, anxiety-building concerns before God in prayer. We can lay them down. We can place our trust in God rather than be ruled and driven by fear.

NARRATIVE ON THE TEXT | The Rest of the Story

The angel of God comes and completely routs the Assyrian army, and they go home. From this point on in history, Assyria goes into a decline from which it never recovers.

As we look back on this biblical account, we realize that Hezekiah was never really alone. He faced hard times and his faith was tested, but God was with him every step of the way. Just as God was with Hezekiah, he wants to be with us. God wants us to avoid the pitfalls of Ahaz. We don't have to live under the tyranny of fear and anxiety. We are called to lives of trust and faith.

All of us have ups and downs. No matter how much we love God and walk with Jesus, we still have moments when anxiety slips in. But through the power of God's Holy Spirit, we can have lives that are predominantly characterized by the peace and freedom that come from God's presence in our lives. That's how God wants us to live.

NEW TESTAMENT CONNECTION

Meeting the God of Peace

God does not want his children living as captives to fear. He offers another path, and prayer is the starting point of our journey from fear to faith.

> Do not be anxious about anything, but in everything, by prayer and petition, with thanksgiving, present your requests to God. And the peace of God, which transcends all understanding, will guard your hearts and your minds in Christ Jesus. (Philippians 4:6–7)

CREATIVE MESSAGE IDEA | Lay It Out

When we face times of anxiety and fear, the single most important activity that we can engage in is prayer. Like Hezekiah, we can come to God and spread out our needs and fears before him. We can admit our anxiety, confusion, and need for him to deliver us.

At this time you can ask everyone to take out the card you gave them as they entered the room. (If you are going to use this creative message idea, you will need to have a card or a blank piece of paper for everyone who is gathered. They will also need a writing utensil.) Invite them to write down a word or sentence that represents a fear that has been gripping and controlling their life. Then, allow a time of silence for each person to bring this fear before God. If your tradition encourages kneeling and if you have space to do so, consider inviting people to take a posture of spreading out before the Lord. After a time of silence, lift up a prayer asking for those gathered to experience freedom and release from the fears that have kept them captive.

SESSION

6

Micah: Doing Justice

ISAIAH 1:13; AMOS 4:1; MICAH 2:11; 3:1; 6:6–8; 7:16–19

The Heart of the MESSAGE

The prophets call us to hear, see, and feel what we would miss on our own. It is easy for our hearts to become calloused and our eyes blinded to the sin in our lives, churches, and culture. The prophets strip away all of the facades and help us see ourselves as we really are.

Micah calls us to a deep level of self-examination and then to transformation. Three words ring out loud and clear: justice, kindness, and humility. God wants more than offerings and religious observance. He wants our hearts to beat in unison with his heart. He wants our lives to reflect the justice he desires to see on this earth. When we hear the voice of God speaking through the prophets and when we respond to his call, we will see our lives, the church, and the world transformed.

Brief Message OUTLINE

1. Why Read the Prophets?
2. The Call of Micah

The Heart of the MESSENGER

The prophets have a deep concern that followers of God not fall into the trap of "being religious" but failing to have a heart that reflects the heart of God. As you prepare to bring this message, take time for self-examination. How can you live in a way that brings God's justice alive in this world? Is your heart tender toward others, and do you show kindness freely? How can you grow in humility? Also, take time to think about your habits as a worshiper. Are you just going through the motions, or are you truly meeting God in worship? Does worship bring transforming power into your life?

SIGNIFICANT SCRIPTURE

Isaiah 1:13; Amos 4:1; Micah 3:1

NARRATIVE ON THE TEXT | Examples of Harsh Prophetic Words

Throughout the Old Testament we get a window into the heart of the prophets. From some of their words, it would be easy to get the feeling that the prophets got up on the wrong side of the bed. Here are just a few samples of why people might see the prophets as a bit cranky:

> Hear this word, you cows of Bashan on Mount Samaria,
> you women who oppress the poor and crush the needy
> and say to your husbands, "Bring us some drinks!"
> (Amos 4:1)

Amos is calling the women of Israel cows! He is saying that they are more concerned about where they will get their next drink than they are about the poor and the needy.

> Stop bringing meaningless offerings!
> Your incense is detestable to me.
> New Moons, Sabbaths and convocations—
> I cannot bear your evil assemblies. (Isaiah 1:13)

Isaiah is telling the people that God is fed up with their offerings, gatherings, and their whole religious lives.

> Listen, you leaders of Jacob,
> you rulers of the house of Israel.
> Should you not know justice,
> you who hate good and love evil;
> who tear the skin from my people
> and the flesh from their bones;

CREATIVE MESSAGE IDEA | The Emotions of the Prophets

Think for a moment about basic human emotions. We all have feelings. Sometimes we are filled with joy; at other times sadness fills our heart. We feel compassion, anger, fear, happiness, and many other emotions. This is just part of being human.

We also tend to associate certain emotions with different groups of people. Invite those gathered to identify what emotion they most often associate with the different groups of people you are going to list. Have everyone tell someone sitting near them two emotions that come to mind when they think of:

- clowns
- police officers
- school principals
- nurses
- prophets

We often begin to characterize a whole group of people and assign a certain emotional state to this group. When it comes to the prophets, it would be easy to see them as stern, angry, and even little depressive.

who eat my people's flesh,
  strip off their skin
  and break their bones in pieces;
who chop them up like meat for the pan,
  like flesh for the pot? (Micah 3:1–3)

Micah is speaking in metaphor, but the message is loud and clear. The people are filled with injustice and the consequences are grave.

If we simply skim through the words of the prophets, we can get the sense that they were a pretty surly and angry bunch.

NARRATIVE ON THE TEXT | Examples of Strange Behavior

Not only did the prophets speak harsh and angry words, their behavior often looked downright bizarre! Here are a few examples:

- *Hosea* marries a prostitute to reveal the broken heart of God over his people who have wandered away from him. Imagine a seminary student or young single pastor announcing to friends and family that he was getting married to a common hooker who was known by everyone in town.
- *Ezekiel* eats food cooked over excrement to create a picture of just how unclean the people have become and to point to how bad the conditions will become for God's people if they do not repent.
- *Jeremiah* digs up a filthy pair of underwear to show people the disgusting nature of their behavior.

Although all of these men were doing exactly what God called them to do, the casual observer would have seen these choices and behaviors as bizarre.

1. Why Read the Prophets?

There are basically three reasons why believers should read what the prophets have written:

- because they are in the Bible
- because they help us hear what we would never hear on our own
- because we need their message to pierce our hearts

We will examine these three reasons in more detail.

NEW TESTAMENT CONNECTION

It Is All from God

Avoiding any part of the Bible is a mistake. The apostle Paul emphasized that the entire Old Testament is God's Word when he wrote to Timothy: "All Scripture is God-breathed and is useful for teaching, rebuking, correcting and training in righteousness, so that the man of God may be thoroughly equipped for every good work" (2 Timothy 3:16–17).

NARRATIVE ON LIFE

Easy to Avoid

First, we read the prophets because they are in the Bible. Let's be honest, it would be easy to avoid reading the prophets. As a matter of fact, many people do exactly that. The prophets hold a mirror up to our soul and show us where we have become marred, scarred, and ugly. They are not really happy books. They tell us things we don't want to hear. They convict us of sin. They remind us that there are serious consequences for rebelling against God. It would be easy to relegate these books of the Old Testament to some kind of secondary status.

If we fall for the temptation to avoid reading the prophets, we do so to our own peril. We need the message the prophets bring. We even need the manner in which they communicate. Sometimes a gentle reminder does not get our attention and it takes a spiritual two-by-four to wake us up!

NARRATIVE ON LIFE

Our Hearts Have Become Numb

Second, we read the prophets because they help us hear what we would never hear on our own. There are many things God wants us to see, but our eyes can be blind. There are truths the Holy Spirit is speaking to us, but we are often spiritually hard-of-hearing. Our hearts have become numb, and we don't always get the subtle promptings of the Holy Spirit. The prophets speak with such conviction and clarity and at such a volume that they break through numb hearts.

ILLUSTRATION

Singing Off-Key

Imagine you are listening to someone sing, but that person is singing off-key—not just a little off-key, way off! Moreover, he or she is doing so at the full volume.

ON THE LIGHTER SIDE

What Will You Say to Malachi?

Just imagine that when you get to heaven, you meet Malachi. This great prophet of Israel asks you, "So, how did you like my book?"

You don't want to have to say, "Oops! I never got around to it. It was in a bad location—you know, way at the end of the Old Testament. It was only four chapters long and didn't seem that significant. I started the Old Testament Challenge, but I got stuck back somewhere in Leviticus and never got to the end of the story."

If you are musically insensitive, such off-key singing won't bother you much. You might notice, but you can live with it. If you have perfect pitch and are a trained musician, however, it's a different story. You notice each note and how it does not fit. You realize how far off pitch this person is. It can be almost painful!

A person with perfect pitch agonizes over the singing not just because it sounds so bad but because he or she realizes how good and beautiful the song could sound. This is the experience of the prophets. God has given them a vision of what could be, and they hear how human beings have gone so far out of tune with God's plan. The prophets see, hear, and feel with God. They know the heart of God and call us to get our lives back in tune.

NARRATIVE ON LIFE | What's the Big Deal?

We tend to look at the world through our own personal filters. If we feel happy and have our needs met, we think the world is a pretty good place. When things are going well for us, we can walk right past things that break the heart of God and not even notice them.

- We look at the world and our society and think that things aren't that bad.
- We hear about violence on the news, but if it does not touch us or those close to us, it does not seem that important.
- We lie a little bit, but we comfort ourselves by thinking that this is common and everyone does it.
- We are unfaithful in thought or action, but we echo the old saying, "What he/she doesn't know won't hurt him/her."
- We cheat in business or school and justify it by saying that everyone does it.
- Eight thousand children and young people are infected with AIDS every single day in sub-Saharan Africa; it is now the leading cause of death in that part of the world, but because it is so far away, we hardly feel a thing.

CREATIVE MESSAGE IDEA | Until It Hurts

Plan to have a trio (of voices or instruments) do a short musical number at this point in the message. Have two of the voices or instruments in tune and together. Have a third that is intentionally, clearly, and loudly out of tune. The number does not have to be long, even one full minute should be enough, but it will feel like eternity! Have them play or sing until it hurts!

NEW TESTAMENT CONNECTION

The Voice of Jesus

The voice of Jesus enters in with the voices of the prophets. He also reminds us that God is very concerned about justice and righteousness. Jesus says:

> Then the King will say to those on his right, "Come, you who are blessed by my Father; take your inheritance, the kingdom prepared for you since the creation of the world. For I was hungry and you gave me something to eat, I was thirsty and you gave me something to drink, I was a stranger and you invited me in, I needed clothes and you clothed me, I was sick and you looked after me, I was in prison and you came to visit me." (Matthew 25:34–36)

If we ever wonder whether the prophets are overstating their case, all we have to do is read these words of Jesus from the gospel of Matthew. Jesus is clear that justice and righteousness matter more than we dream.

- People in our country live on the streets and go to sleep with empty stomachs, and we learn to walk past them and look the other way. We convince ourselves that it is probably their own fault and they deserve the plight they are in.
- Someone shades the truth to close a business deal and make a few more bucks and we say, "That's just how business goes!"
- We get a little wrapped up in our own comfort, focus more and more on our needs, and quickly forget the needs of the poor and outcast.
- We get the paycheck we worked so hard for and don't even think to give back to the God who has provided all that we have.

These things happen every day, every moment, and we say, "What's the big deal? That's life!"

The prophets, on the other hand, act as if the world is falling apart. They get all stressed out and seem to think that these things are a much bigger deal than we ever thought. The prophets echo the heart of God, who sees and cares about all of these things. The prophets wake us up to the fact that all of these things are a bigger deal than we would have ever guessed!

INTERPRETIVE INSIGHT | The Burden of the Prophets

The prophets bear the crushing burden of feeling what God feels, seeing what God sees, and hearing what God hears. Their passion is the natural extension of God's call on their lives. Their seemingly bizarre behavior begins to make sense when we understand the depth of their pain over sin. They are giving a human voice to the divine cry of a God who is broken over the depth of sin in our world and the life-crushing injustices that happen every day but no one seems to notice.

The rich get richer and the poor get poorer. Lies are spoken and no one seems to notice or care. Dishonest business practices have become normative and we look the other way, as if it does not matter. Prisoners sit day after day in jail and no one visits them. Children go to bed hungry while their neighbors feast and feel no sorrow for the poor around them. God sees all of this, God feels, and he shares his heart through the words of the prophets.

NARRATIVE ON LIFE | The Battle of the Prophets

Third, we read the prophets because we need their message to pierce our hearts. Prophet after prophet learned that people don't really want to know the truth about sin and what it has done to our lives, society, and world. Hearing the voice of the prophets and seeing the broken heart of God make us uncomfortable. It is easier to live with blind eyes, deaf ears, and hard hearts.

Time and time again throughout the Old Testament the prophets come with stern warnings from God. They come to help the people see, hear, and feel with God. Over and over the people reject them. Sometimes the people laugh, at other times they mock, and at still other times they simply walk away. Sadly, there are also times when the people lash out in anger. Prophets are beaten, imprisoned, and even killed!

Today the response to the prophets tends to be a little tamer. Most people simply avoid them. The voices of the prophets still cry out. They still help to pierce our hearts with the truth of God. The question is, Will we fight and resist, or will we receive the words of the prophets with humility?

NARRATIVE ON THE TEXT | The Effect of Beer or Wine

Here is a question to ask everyone gathered: What is the effect of drinking beer or wine? Does it make a person more alert and sharp, or does it make them more comfortable and relaxed? (Ask people to respond out loud.)

In general, drinking alcohol causes people to become mellow, relaxed, and less focused. In Micah 2:11 the prophet is making a powerful statement about the condition of the human heart. He says that people prefer to live in a state of spiritual inebriation. We don't want to notice, we prefer not to feel, and we would rather not hear about all the pain in the world. If a prophet came who brought words that made us feel comfortable, mellow, and relaxed, we would love this prophet.

The problem is, prophets speak the words of God. The truth of God often convicts and makes us feel uncomfortable. God's truth challenges us and moves us to action.

SIGNIFICANT SCRIPTURE

Micah 2:11

ILLUSTRATION | Just Turn on the TV

Imagine it is 7:00 in the evening and you are about to sit down in front of the TV to unwind. You figure you will channel surf around the hundred-plus options you have as a result of your new satellite system. Then, there is a knock on the front door. You open the door and are shocked to find Micah, Amos, and Isaiah standing there! You invite them in and you all sit down together for an evening of prime-time channel surfing. Over the next five hours these three prophets watch as you view short clips from some of the following categories:

- talk shows (from Oprah to Jerry Springer)
- reality TV shows

The shallowness of our moral comprehension, the incapacity to sense the depth of misery caused by our own failures, is a simple fact of fallen humanity which no explanation can cover up.
ABRAHAM HESCHEL

PAUSE FOR REFLECTION

Hearing the Prophets

The prophets really do speak for God. They see what he sees. They feel what he feels. They express the heart of God with a human voice and help us see what we often want to avoid. We omit them from our reading of Scripture at great cost and risk to our own souls!

Take a brief time of silence and ask the Holy Spirit to soften your heart to hear the words of the prophets. Also, invite the Spirit to reveal areas in your life where you have become numb to sin. Spend a few moments reflecting on your own life and the transformation God wants to bring.

The prophet is a man who feels fiercely. God has thrust a burden upon his soul, and he is bowed and stunned at man's fierce greed. Prophecy is the voice God has lent to the silent agony. . . . God is raging in the prophet's words.

Abraham Heschel

- HBO and Showtime special programming
- sporting events
- situation comedies (from reruns of *Leave It to Beaver* to *Will and Grace*)
- dramas (police, drama, hospital)
- infomercials and TV shopping malls
- news programs
- late night shows

You even give them a sample of some of the special adult pay-to-view channels.

How might these prophets respond to the smorgasbord of viewing options that are commonplace in our world today? If they were sitting with you and interacting about these shows, how might your perspective on these shows change?

NARRATIVE ON LIFE | Becoming Too Comfortable

Events that horrified the prophets have become everyday occurrences in our world. Things that the prophets condemned in the name of God have become standard business practice and normal operating procedures in the marketplace today. Attitudes that brought condemnation from the prophets are tolerated in our society and often in our local churches. We have become so comfortable and complacent that we hardly notice the presence of sin all around us.

It is like a necklace or ring that feels strange when we first put it on. After a short time, we don't even notice it. Or, it is like a broken item around the house. It bugs us at first, but with time, it just blends in. We don't even see it anymore. With time, things that should bother us and break our hearts can become part of our landscape of life. The job of the prophets is to get our attention and help us notice what we have forgotten.

ILLUSTRATION | Welcome to the Hog Farm

Have you ever driven by a hog farm? If you have, you know it! As you get close to the farm, you are hit with a wall of stench that is distinct to this kind of animal. If it happens to be a warm and damp day, it can be even more intense. You may find yourself wondering, "How can anyone live close to a hog farm? How can they tolerate the smell?" But, if you actually stay near the hog farm for a few hours, something amazing happens. The smell goes away!

Well, it does not really go away, but you stop noticing it. Somehow, your mind and senses make adjustments. With time, the smell is not nearly as intense. Then, if you stay long enough, it seems to disappear. If you were to leave for a time and come back, you would notice the smell again, but you would also adjust again.

Sin functions in a similar way. With time, if we stay in close proximity to certain sinful practices, we don't notice the smell, we don't see the consequences, and we can't see what the big deal is anyway. It is the job of the prophets to shake us, wake us, and help us realize that something stinks!

2. The Call of Micah

NARRATIVE ON THE TEXT | Notice the Escalation

In Micah 6:6–8, the prophet begins by asking a fundamental question: What can I bring to God? What does he really want from me? He then forms a list of possible answers to this question. Notice how Micah begins small and then escalates.

- "Shall I come . . . with burnt offerings?" Micah begins small. A burnt offering could be a dove or a pigeon, which anyone could afford.
- "Shall I come . . . with calves a year old?" A calf was an expensive gift. Many families could not afford this kind of an offering. This would have been very generous.
- "Will the LORD be pleased with thousands of rams?" This was an offering that only a king could give. The wealthiest person in all the land might be able to muster up this kind of an offering, but it was almost beyond imagination.
- "Will the LORD be pleased . . . with ten thousand rivers of oil?" This was simply impossible. Micah has now escalated the discussion to the point of being ridiculous. No person could offer God even one river of oil, much less ten thousand.
- "Shall I offer my firstborn for my transgression?" Micah knows that human sacrifice is forbidden by God. He is not advocating human sacrifice in any way, shape, or form. He is simply escalating the discussion. He is saying, Would God want me to give my child, that which is most precious to me in this world? Micah is pushing the discussion as far as he can.

The central message of this part of the passage is that none of these things is really what God wants us to offer to him. What God wants is *us!* He wants our hearts and lives fully yielded to him. What God asks for is something anyone can give. He wants us to act in ways that reflect his justice. He invites us to love what

SIGNIFICANT SCRIPTURE

Micah 6:6-8

PAUSE FOR PRAYER

Soften My Heart

Pray for each person to hear the words God speaks through the prophets. Pray in three specific directions:

- *Open our eyes:* Ask the Spirit to open our eyes to see where sin has crept in and gone unnoticed.
- *Open our ears:* Ask God to sensitize the hearing of each person to receive what God wants to say through his prophets.
- *Soften our hearts:* Pray for hearts that are consistently tender and ready for transformation.

is merciful. And God wants us to walk in authentic humility with him. If we are humble before God, we will follow him, and our whole life will be his. This is what God wants from each of his children.

NARRATIVE ON THE TEXT | Do Justice

CREATIVE VIDEO ELEMENT

(VHS or DVD)

Music video, *Doing Justice* (1:30 min.)
Shows imagery of a man sitting alone on a busy street as people walk by.

The prophet Micah continues:

> He has showed you, O man, what is good.
> And what does the LORD require of you?
> To *act justly* and to love mercy
> and to walk humbly with your God. (Micah 6:8)

Justice is a strange thing. We all want it when it comes to us. We long for justice when we have been wronged. We cry "unfair" and expect justice to prevail.

NARRATIVE ON LIFE | Beware of the Double Standard

We all hate it when someone treats us unfairly. If we are wronged, we expect, we even demand, justice. The problem is that most of us live with a double standard. We want justice when it comes to us, but we forget to extend justice to others. We need to ask God to help us be just as concerned and get just as energized over the injustices others suffer. In particular, we need to learn to be concerned over the specific injustices we might be most likely to overlook. God calls us to be his agents of justice in this world.

ON THE LIGHTER SIDE | Swing at Everything!

A story is told by a former referee and umpire. His story is a great reminder of how we all want moments where we can experience justice. This is how he tells the story:

I was driving too fast in the snow in Boulder, Colorado. A policeman pulled me over and gave me a speeding ticket. I tried to talk him out of it. I told him that I was worried about my insurance costs. I tried to explain what a good and careful driver I am. He told me that if I didn't like it, I could go to court.

The first game of the next baseball season I showed up to umpire. As I stood behind home plate, the first batter walked up. I was surprised to see it was the same policeman who gave me the ticket that winter. Our eyes met. He recognized me, and I recognized him. There was an awkward pause.

He asked me, "How did that thing with the ticket go?"

I paused, looked at him, and said, "Swing at everything!"

LIFE APPLICATION | What Can One Person Do?

We cannot correct all of the injustice in the world, but we can all do something. There are some first steps that will move a follower of Christ toward a deeper life of justice. Consider taking a step forward in one of the following ways:

Notice: Ask God to help you tune in and notice injustice around you. This can be painful and cause discomfort, but it is critical for all who want to do justice. We must first learn to take note of where injustice exists. Part of this process is learning to notice where we are part of the injustice problem. When we see this, we need to come before God and humbly seek his power to change.

Pray: Every follower of Christ needs to learn the importance of praying for justice and against injustice. There is amazing power in prayer, and this is a critical starting point for Christ-followers.

Changed behavior: God can help us learn to treat others fairly. Before we go seeking world justice, we need to be sure we are treating the people around us with equity and justice. If God shows you an area where you are being unjust in your treatment of another person, it is time to make some behavior and attitude adjustments.

Courage: We can begin to live with courage in how we relate to others. When we see injustice, we can begin to say something and do something about it. If there are patterns of injustice in our home, at our school, in our workplace, or in our neighborhood, we can learn to enter in and make a difference. This takes courage because we know how people responded to the biblical prophets. We have to be ready for people to resist what we say if we begin calling for justice and righteousness.

Generosity: If we have more than we need—and most of us do—we can begin to share with those who have needs. We can do it on our own as we become aware of needs around us. We can also give through our church or other Christian organizations that provide for the basic needs of the poor.

PAUSE FOR REFLECTION

Learning to Notice

Take time to reflect on where there might be injustice in specific areas of life. Invite people to think honestly and deeply about the possible presence of injustice in their sphere of influence. Can you identify any injustice:

- in how you treat members of your family?
- in your local community?
- in the larger community where you live?
- in your workplace?
- in your local church?
- in how you relate to your neighbors?

ILLUSTRATION | Can I Give It Away?

A mother and son were walking down a city street on a cold winter night. The little boy noticed a man huddled in an alley with only an old blanket to shelter him from the cold. He had never seen this sort of thing before. The mother was concerned for her son and began to pull him away from the situation. He resisted and asked if they could stop. The mother was anxious, but willing to pause for just a moment. Her son motioned for her to lean over so he could say something. He whispered, "I have three more jackets at home, can I give that man my jacket?" His mother looked at him with surprise and concern. She paused and said . . .

How would you finish this story? How do you think it should be finished? What would you have said if you were the mother?

If our goods are not available to the community they are stolen goods.
MARTIN LUTHER

The little boy knew he had three more jackets at home, and he wanted to share. He wanted to help someone who was cold. He had the means to do it. The way we respond in situations like this teaches the next generation about justice.

ILLUSTRATION | An Example of Lavish Loving-Kindness

In a town called Paradise, in California, lives a young man named John Gilbert. When he was five years old, John was diagnosed with Duchenne's Muscular Dystrophy. It was genetic, progressive, and cruel. He was told that it would eventually destroy every muscle in his body. In about ten years this dreadful disease would take his life.

Each year John lost something. One year it was his ability to run; he could no longer play games or sports with other kids. Another year he could no longer walk straight. All he could do was watch other kids play.

John writes that junior high was perhaps the hardest time of his life because other children teased him mercilessly. He was bullied and humiliated until he was afraid to go to school. No one ever stood up for him; maybe they were afraid for themselves and the possible repercussions.

One year John was named the ambassador for Muscular Dystrophy in California. A fund-raising auction was to be held at a big dinner, and John was invited to be a guest for this gathering. It was a highlight for this boy who had experienced so many low-lights in his life. There were actually some NFL stars there who let John hold their massive Superbowl rings.

When the auction began, one item particularly caught John's attention. It was a basketball signed by the Sacramento Kings. John got a little carried away and raised his hand to bid on the ball. He didn't have any money and could never have afforded it, but he was so excited that he bid anyway. When his mom saw his hand go up, she reacted with lightning quickness and pulled his hand down. John later said, "Astronauts never felt as many G's as my wrist did that night!"

The bidding for that basketball went on and on, and the price went up and up! Eventually one man offered an amount that shocked the whole room. No one else could match it. He walked to the front and collected his prize. But instead of returning to his seat, he walked across the room and placed the ball in John's frail, thin hands.

That man placed the very expensive ball into hands that would never dribble a ball down a basketball court, never throw a ball to a teammate for a fast break, and never fire a three-point shot at the buzzer in the hopes of winning a big game.

Have you bought a basketball for anybody lately?

WORD STUDY

Hesed

The second phrase that Micah talks about in Micah 6:8 is to "love mercy." The Hebrew word used here is *hesed*. *Hesed* is the word most closely associated with God's loving-kindness expressed in covenant relationship. It is a love that always seeks to express itself in action toward another individual.

LIFE APPLICATION | First Steps

Living in a way that expresses loving mercy begins with first steps. There are many starting points, but here are a few ideas to get the wheels turning. Maybe you could:

- Sign up to help in the church nursery and give care to a little one who can't say thanks but who needs the tender love you can give while the family is off to worship.
- Serve at a soup kitchen once a month.
- Volunteer to help in the youth ministry of the church. Some of the young people who have experienced the same sort of merciless teasing as John did could use the kind words and sensitivity you could bring to their life.
- Give an unexpected love gift to your spouse.
- Show up for a blood drive and give the gift of blood to a person you will never meet—even if you are terrified of needles.
- Slow down on your high school campus long enough to notice that new kid whom everybody is walking right past. It could be a warm smile and an invitation for him or her to sit with you at lunch.
- Become part of the calling team at church and commit to visit the shut-ins, who can't gather for worship with the community of God's people.
- Offer to help a neighbor who just had a baby and doesn't have a church family to help through the transition time.

There is a loftier ambition than merely to stand high in the world. It is to stoop down and lift mankind higher.
HENRY VAN DYKE

Whatever the first step might be, God wants us to take it. Then, he invites us to a whole lifetime of taking steps that express his tender love and mercy.

NARRATIVE ON THE TEXT | A Fine Line

The final phrase of Micah in Micah 6:8 is to "walk humbly with your God." It is hard to be a prophet and not get a little self-righteous. There is an important theological distinction between being a prophet and being a jerk. As we study the Old Testament, we discover that what burns most deeply in the heart of a true prophet is not anger, it is love. That is because the prophets' hearts beat with the heart of God, and his heart beats with love. The prophets always remember that they too are sinful people. They too need the grace of God. They have to live with humility, even as they call people to beware of their pride and to be humble before God.

NARRATIVE ON THE TEXT | God's Grace

At the close of the book of Micah, we see the grace of God come shining through. Micah declares who God is and unveils the loving heart of the Father:

> Who is a God like you,
> who pardons sin and forgives the transgression
> of the remnant of his inheritance?
> You do not stay angry forever
> but delight to show mercy.
> You will again have compassion on us;
> you will tread our sins underfoot
> and hurl all our iniquities into the depths of the sea.

SIGNIFICANT SCRIPTURE

Micah 7:16-19

PAUSE FOR PRAYER

May God's Will Be Done

In the Lord's Prayer Jesus teaches his followers to pray:

> . . . your kingdom come,
> your will be done
> on earth as it is in heaven.
> (Matthew 6:10)

Followers of Christ often pray for God's will to be done. Micah helps us see what such a lifestyle will look like. His will is done when we do justice, love mercy, and walk humbly with God. Close by praying for these three things to become realities in the lives of all who follow Jesus.

NEW TESTAMENT CONNECTION | The Call to Humility

All through the Bible, followers of Christ are called to live humbly. In most cases, there is also a warning about the danger of pride. This theme is strong and clear in the New Testament:

> All of you, clothe yourselves with humility toward one another, because,
>
> "God opposes the proud
> but gives grace to the humble."
>
> Humble yourselves, therefore, under God's mighty hand, that he may lift you up in due time. Cast all your anxiety on him because he cares for you. (1 Peter 5:5-7)

> But he gives us more grace. That is why Scripture says:
>
> "God opposes the proud
> but gives grace to the humble."
>
> Submit yourselves, then, to God. Resist the devil, and he will flee from you. Come near to God and he will come near to you. . . . Humble yourselves before the Lord, and he will lift you up. (James 4:6-10)

> Be completely humble and gentle; be patient, bearing with one another in love. (Ephesians 4:2)

SESSION 7

Jeremiah: When God Gives a Hard Assignment

JEREMIAH 1–37; LAMENTATIONS 3:21–26

The Heart of the MESSAGE

Some people teach that following God leads to a safe, painless life. They tell us that if we are faithful to God's call, we will have protection from suffering and things will go our way. These folks have never met a prophet named Jeremiah.

Jeremiah lived with a heart that was humbly yielded to God. He heard the voice of the Father call him to proclaim the word of the Lord, and he lived with a tenacious obedience to this calling. But his faithfulness was met with resistance. His preaching was discarded and ignored. As he humbly followed God, he was mocked, rejected, beaten, imprisoned, and left to rot in a hole in the ground.

In the life of Jeremiah we learn that sometimes God calls his children to a hard assignment. Our responsibility is to follow, even through pain and tears.

The Heart of the MESSENGER

Every follower of Christ will experience moments of struggle and pain. We can be right in the center of God's will knowing it is the right place to be, but it may be a hard place. Take time to reflect on your past. How have you experienced God's presence, care, and strength revealed in the midst of a hard time? When have you been obedient to God's call and discovered that it was a hard place to be? You might even be in such a place right now.

Ask God to help you communicate with humble honesty. Many of those gathered will be in the midst of a painful time of their life. They may be walking the road that Jeremiah walked. Ask God to prepare your heart as you bring this sobering message that being in God's will does not always mean a painless existence. Also pray that God will use you to help people see that hard assignments can bring them closer to God more than almost anything else.

Brief Message OUTLINE

1. The Beginning of Jeremiah's Ministry —A Strong Start
2. Jeremiah Faces Reality—Pain Sets In
3. Jeremiah's Enduring Spirit—Hanging in There
4. A Word for Those Who Don't Walk Jeremiah's Road—Seek Balance

1. The Beginning of Jeremiah's Ministry—A Strong Start

SIGNIFICANT SCRIPTURE
Jeremiah 1:4–10, 17–19

NARRATIVE ON THE TEXT | The Call of Jeremiah

God's call to Jeremiah is loud and clear. Anyone who wonders if Jeremiah is on the right track has failed to read his story. God lets Jeremiah know that his call came from the first moment of his conception:

> "Before I formed you in the womb I knew you,
> before you were born I set you apart;
> I appointed you as a prophet to the nations."
> (Jeremiah 1:5)

Jeremiah, like many of us, feels as if he is not up to the task. He has a healthy understanding of his own frailness and wonders if he can fulfill God's plan for his life. He cries out, "Ah, Sovereign LORD. . . . I do not know how to speak; I am only a child" (Jeremiah 1:6).

God reassures Jeremiah and lets him know that his abilities and strength are not the primary issue. His job is to follow God's leading and speak the words God has called him to proclaim. God says to Jeremiah: "Do not say, 'I am only a child.' You must go to everyone I send you to and say whatever I command you. Do not be afraid of them, for I am with you and will rescue you" (Jeremiah 1:7–8).

Finally, God gives Jeremiah a hint of what lies ahead in his ministry. When we read these words, we get a sense that Jeremiah is not heading out on a journey that will be smooth and easy. God tells him:

> "Get yourself ready! Stand up and say to them whatever I command you. Do not be terrified by them, or I will terrify you before them. Today I have made you a fortified city, an iron pillar and a bronze wall to stand against the whole land—against the kings of Judah, its officials, its priests and the people of the land. They will fight against you but will not overcome you, for I am with you and will rescue you." (Jeremiah 1:17–19)

SIGNIFICANT SCRIPTURE
Jeremiah 2–19

NARRATIVE ON LIFE | And They're Off!

When we move into Jeremiah 2 and the chapters that follow, we watch him bolt from the starting blocks. He starts the race with passion and intensity. He is a young man, full of energy and optimism. He loves having a mission and a purpose for his life. Every indication is that Jeremiah leaves the gate running full speed ahead!

We can almost hear him saying to himself, "I'm going to speak the words of God to whoever he tells me to speak them to. No matter how much it costs me, I will fulfill my calling." Jeremiah is deeply committed to the call God has placed on his life. He is ready to run the race with all the strength he has.

Most followers of Christ can point back to some point in their spiritual life where they felt as Jeremiah at the start of his ministry. There was a time when God got hold of us and gave us a mission—a calling. It may have been during a camp experience as a young person. We felt God's call and said, "Wherever you lead, I will follow." Maybe it happened in a church service where the Holy Spirit spoke in power and we said, "Take my life; it is yours—100 percent!" Maybe it was in a quiet moment of personal devotional study. We opened the Word and God spoke in a clear way. We were moved to say, "From this day on, I will serve you and use my gifts to further the work of your kingdom."

At some point along the way in our journey of faith we had a clear sense that the transcendent God was inviting us into his grand redemptive drama. We realized that God was orchestrating our involvement in plans for redeeming our fallen world. Like Jeremiah, we were overwhelmed that God would call us. But we were willing to say "Yes."

With deep conviction and commitment we charged out of the starting blocks to run the race that God set before us. We purposed in our hearts to run hard and to run fast. We committed ourselves to run faithfully all the way to the end and to run for the glory of the One whose name we bear.

2. Jeremiah Faces Reality—Pain Sets In

NARRATIVE ON THE TEXT | A Tough Start

From Jeremiah 2 through 19, the prophet is speaking the words of God. He is being faithful. He's doing the work. Sadly, the people don't respond the way Jeremiah hopes. The people are not responsive to any of his messages. They are clearly resistant. Like any communicator, Jeremiah longs that people will hear, be touched, and respond. But it seems as if Jeremiah's words are hitting deaf ears and hard hearts.

So, in chapter 19, God calls Jeremiah to turn up the heat. He gives him an illustration, a picture to help the people get the point.

> This is what the LORD says: "Go and buy a clay jar from a potter. Take along some of the elders of the people and of the priests . . . and say, 'Hear the word of the LORD, O kings of Judah

> and people of Jerusalem. This is what the LORD Almighty, the God of Israel, says: Listen! I am going to bring a disaster on this place that will make the ears of everyone who hears of it tingle. For they have forsaken me and made this a place of foreign gods; they have burned sacrifices in it to gods that neither they nor their fathers nor the kings of Judah ever knew, and they have filled this place with the blood of the innocent. . . . '
>
> "Then break the jar while those who go with you are watching, and say to them, 'This is what the LORD Almighty says: I will smash this nation and this city just as this potter's jar is smashed and cannot be repaired. They will bury the dead in Topheth until there is no more room.'" (Jeremiah 19:1–4, 10–11)

CREATIVE VIDEO ELEMENT

(VHS or DVD)

When God Gives a Hard Assignment (4:30 min.) This interview helps illustrate Jeremiah's life as we see how someone continues to follow God's call even though the assignment is hard.

Jeremiah buys a jar, under the direction of God, and uses it to show the people of Judah what is coming if they do not repent and turn from their wicked ways. He stands in front of all the leaders of the nation of Judah and says, "I'm telling you one last time, 'Humble yourself before God. Stop worshiping foreign gods. Reduce your pride. Open your hearts to his leading and prompting.' And if you don't, watch closely now!" Then Jeremiah smashes the jar.

SIGNIFICANT SCRIPTURE

Jeremiah 20–37

NARRATIVE ON THE TEXT | A Bad Day in Ministry

We don't have to wait long to discover how people feel about Jeremiah's preaching and his "broken jar" illustration. In Jeremiah 20:1–2 we read, "When the priest . . . heard Jeremiah prophesying these things, he had Jeremiah the prophet beaten and put in the stocks at the Upper Gate of Benjamin at the LORD's temple." He is left there, right by the temple for everyone to see and mock. He is not released until the next morning. It is safe to say that his ministry is not well received.

CREATIVE MESSAGE IDEA | A Shattered Jar

God is seeking to communicate, through Jeremiah, that the people are in a dangerous place. If you read Jeremiah 19:1–15 closely, you will discover that their sins have become so detestable that God is saying, "It is decision time. It's now or never!" The jar becomes a picture of a level of brokenness that cannot be repaired.

The look and sound of the jar being smashed would have shocked the people of Judah. To help create the same kind of feeling, find a large clay pot and have it displayed prominently as people are entering for worship. While you are talking about a clay jar, hold it in your hands. People will begin wondering if you are actually going to smash it.

When you talk about Jeremiah smashing the jar, drop it, or hit it with a hammer. Let the sight and sound sink in before you say anything. Then talk about how this would have made the people of Judah feel. Jeremiah is clear that the jar represents their nation. He smashes it and tells them that this is the future of Judah if things do not change. Imagine how they feel toward him at that moment.

This is a very bad day in Jeremiah's ministry. It's one thing when your ministry doesn't go along very well—people aren't responsive, there aren't breakthroughs, and there aren't miraculous answers to prayer. It is entirely another thing when you take a physical beating and face public shame just for doing what God has called you to do.

Jeremiah never thought this would happen to him. God promised: "I will be with you. I will protect you. I will rescue you." But Jeremiah doesn't feel the presence of God at this moment. He feels abandoned. He has been beaten mercilessly and then is spread out and put in the stocks for the night. Can you imagine what is going through the prophet's mind as the night wears on, his wounds bleed, his body aches, and the people continue to taunt him?

NEW TESTAMENT CONNECTION

Paul's Words to His Friend Timothy

The apostle Paul wrote to his good friend Timothy. Timothy was a young pastor who had started out strong and excited but had become somewhat disillusioned along the way. Some people did not respect him because he was young. Others just outright resisted his ministry. But in the midst of it all, Paul reminded Timothy of the lesson Jeremiah had learned so many years before:

> You, however, know all about my teaching, my way of life, my purpose, faith, *patience*, love, *endurance*, *persecutions, sufferings*—what kinds of things happened to me in Antioch, Iconium and Lystra, the *persecutions I endured*. Yet the Lord rescued me from all of them. In fact, *everyone who wants to live a godly life in Christ Jesus will be persecuted*." (2 Timothy 3:10–12, italics added)

NARRATIVE ON LIFE | There Will Be Hard Days

Like Jeremiah, all who follow Jesus and seek to obey his calling will discover that there are hard days along the way. Some may face only a few days of pain, sorrow, and rejection related to their commitment to follow the Savior. Others may experience far more times of rejection and sorrow. But for all who hear the call and follow, there will be hard times to face.

Many of us start out strong and run the race with excitement. Then, with time, we discover that ministry has its own particular demands, people are not always appreciative, and the seeds we sow don't always spring up into a harvest overnight. We learn that patience and long-suffering are part of doing God's will in this world. With time, we hit a point where we have to decide to keep running the race, even when it gets hard.

NARRATIVE ON THE TEXT | Commitment through the Pain

Jeremiah is not afraid to tell God how he feels about all he is facing. He feels tricked, deceived, discouraged, and beaten up. We look at Jeremiah, and the fresh-faced young buck who ran so hard at the start of his ministry appears ragged and tired:

> O LORD, you deceived me, and I was deceived;
> you overpowered me and prevailed.
> I am ridiculed all day long;
> everyone mocks me.
> Whenever I speak, I cry out
> proclaiming violence and destruction.
> So the word of the LORD has brought me
> insult and reproach all day long. (Jeremiah 20:7–8)

Be not miserable about what may happen tomorrow. The same everlasting Father, who cares for you today, will care for you tomorrow and every day. Either He will shield you from suffering or He will give you unfailing strength to bear it.
FRANCIS DE SALES

Yet, from the depths of his pain and sorrow, Jeremiah's heart shows through. Although he has been beaten, rejected, mocked, scorned, and openly humiliated, he is still ready to follow the God who formed him in his mother's womb and called him from his childhood. In the midst of unspeakable rejection and back-breaking discouragement, Jeremiah cries out:

> But if I say, "I will not mention him
> or speak any more in his name,"
> his word is in my heart like a fire,
> a fire shut up in my bones.
> I am weary of holding it in;
> indeed, I cannot. (Jeremiah 20:9)

In other words, Jeremiah says, "Even if I wanted to stop speaking for God, I can't! His truth is like a fire burning in my soul. I must speak for God! I must do my ministry. I will press on." What an example of tenacious faithfulness in the furnace of life.

NARRATIVE ON THE TEXT | When Things Go from Bad to Worse

As we read Jeremiah 20–37, we see the faithful prophet going out and speaking God's words again and again. The fire that burns in him propels him through beatings, rejection, and discouragement out into ministry again. We may find ourselves hoping that this time the people will respond. Maybe they will see Jeremiah's courage and listen to the words God is speaking through him. Maybe this time they will get the message. Maybe the lesson of the broken clay jar will sink in and they will respond.

ON THE LIGHTER SIDE | Shocking Irony

One day, Jeremiah is brought from the filth of the dungeon to the king's palace. He faces Zedekiah, king of Judah, and is asked one question. It is almost humorous, in light of all Jeremiah has gone through. The king asks him, "Is there any word from the LORD?"

Jeremiah must have stood there in shock. He has been speaking God's word for years now. He has been proclaiming it over and over. But no one has wanted to hear it. Now the king wants a private meeting with the least popular man in all of Jerusalem. The king wants to know if Jeremiah has a word from God.

Zedekiah is certainly looking for good news, something encouraging. But Jeremiah waits on the Lord, hears him speak, and passes the message on to the king. Here it is: "You will be handed over to the king of Babylon" (Jeremiah 37:17). Jeremiah may have hoped that he could give one piece of good news at this moment. But God calls Jeremiah to inform the king that he will be handed over to the ruler of the nation they fear the most. What a shocking irony!

Sadly, the exact opposite happens. Jeremiah is beaten again and is then thrown into a dungeon for a long time (Jeremiah 37:15–16). This ministry to which God has called Jeremiah is hard and getting harder. Jeremiah cannot figure out why things are turning out this way. This is not what he signed up for. This is not how he thought it was going to turn out. He actually comes to the point that he feels if he stays imprisoned, he will die (Jeremiah 37:20).

Nothing is really lost by a life of sacrifice; everything is lost by a failure to obey God's call.

HENRY PARRY LIDDEN

NARRATIVE ON THE TEXT | Things Can't Get Any Worse, Can They?

Jeremiah, remarkably, continues to speak the words of God after two beatings, being put in stocks, and being thrown in a dungeon. In response to his continued ministry and preaching, Jeremiah is thrown into a cistern. We read that he is lowered with a rope into a cistern filled with mud and that his enemies are going to leave him there until he dies (Jeremiah 38:7–9).

Later, Jeremiah's friends find out that he's been put in that cistern and bargain for his release. With time, they are able to pull him out with ropes, clean him up, and set him free. Take a wild guess at what Jeremiah does when he is released from his death sentence in the cistern. He goes out yet again and declares the words of God to the people who have resisted and rejected him!

3. Jeremiah's Enduring Spirit—Hanging in There

NARRATIVE ON LIFE | Forty Years Down the Drain?

Jeremiah's relentless preaching seems to make no impact on the people of Judah. They refuse to listen to his warnings, and just as Jeremiah prophesied, the Babylonian army comes and conquers Jerusalem. They destroy the city, break down the walls, and desecrate the temple. The people of Judah are taken into captivity, as prisoners of war, to Babylon.

HISTORICAL CONTEXT | A Little Information about Cisterns

In ancient days in Israel, water was life. This was a desert land with little water available. If a home or city ran out of water, it was a major crisis. Thus, the people built cisterns. These were different from wells. Wells were a natural source of underground water. Cisterns were a man-made means of catching and saving rainwater.

When a storm came, the rains would fall hard and then wash away or be assimilated into the ground. The people discovered that they could dig down and make large cisterns to capture the water and keep it for long periods of time.

When cisterns were abandoned, they were smelly, awful places, teeming with insects and leeches and often dead animals. They could become a breeding place for all kinds of disease. We don't know the exact condition of the cistern Jeremiah was lowered into, but we can be sure it was not a pleasant place.

Shortly after the fall of Jerusalem, Jeremiah realizes that what he has spent the last forty years of his life trying to avert has just happened. He could have looked at all he suffered—the humiliations, beatings, intimidation, prison time, and the whole cistern ordeal—and feel as if it is all for nothing. He also could have looked at all the hours of preaching, waiting on the Lord, and interacting with the nation of Judah as a waste.

In the same way, we can get discouraged when we try to accomplish God's purposes and face resistance. We can feel as if our devotion and faithfulness have yielded nothing. We can look back and think that all our prayers, effort, and ministry have made no difference at all.

But, like Jeremiah, we must learn that God does not measure success the same way we do. Our faithfulness in following his leading matters to God, even if we don't see the fruit of our work. We also need to have confidence that God sees the impact of our lives with a wide-angle lens. God saw the impact of Jeremiah's life in his day, and he sees the impact Jeremiah is still having today! Jeremiah could not see the big picture. In the same way, we can trust that God will use our ministry even when we cannot see the results immediately.

LIFE APPLICATION | A Time to Weep

In the book of Ecclesiastes we are told that there is a time for everything. The writer says, among other things, that there is:

> a time to weep and a time to laugh,
> a time to mourn and a time to dance. (Ecclesiastes 3:4)

Jeremiah learns that tears are often appropriate. In particular, when the heart of God is broken, our hearts should break as well. When we see people who resist God and run from his grace, we should be sad, even as God is sad. When we see sin in our lives, tears are appropriate—and these tears should lead to change! Jeremiah teaches us that there are times when tears and mourning are the right response.

HISTORICAL CONTEXT | The Birthplace of Lamentations

When you know the story of Jeremiah, you begin to understand why he has been nicknamed "The Weeping Prophet." Later in his life, after the fall of Jerusalem, Jeremiah writes the book of Lamentations. This book is a reflection on how God feels about what happened to Jerusalem and his people. It also seems to express the heart of Jeremiah, the man who did all he could to call the people to a place of repentance so that they would not have to face the invasion of Babylon and the destruction of the holy city.

Those who have received a difficult assignment from God need to pull up a chair at the feet of Jeremiah. From the vantage point of the casual observer, Jeremiah's whole ministry can look like a total bust. He preached his heart out for four decades, and nobody ever responded. He warned, pleaded, prayed, and smashed jars, and no one repented. Jeremiah's ministry never went the way he envisioned. Yet he wept, looked back to God, and continued on.

INTERPRETIVE INSIGHT | Messy Prayer

Jeremiah is disillusioned, frustrated, and angry. He doesn't know what to do with all of his disillusionment. Like the rest of us, he is certainly tempted to stuff it down inside and ignore it. He may have been tempted to put on a happy face, pretend it doesn't bother him, or even quit. Rather than these more common responses, Jeremiah does something few God-fearing people have the courage to do: He spills his guts out to God.

SIGNIFICANT SCRIPTURE
Jeremiah 20

In the midst of his pain, Jeremiah lifts up one of the messiest prayers recorded in all of Scripture. We looked at the basic content of this prayer earlier, but now we need to dig into the heart of it.

- *Jeremiah accuses God of tricking him.* He says, "You deceived me" (Jeremiah 20:7). The root word here means that Jeremiah feels seduced under false pretenses. He is saying to God, "You pulled a bait-and-switch. You indicated to me that my ministry was going to be exciting, that you were going to accompany me on this adventure, and that you were going to protect me. That's not the way it's turning out." Jeremiah pours out honest frustration.
- *Jeremiah tells God that his life and ministry don't make sense.* He says, "I've had it about up to here with speaking your words and getting no results. The end result that I see is only more negative responses from people" (Jeremiah 20:7–8).
- *Jeremiah curses the day he was born* (Jeremiah 20:14–15). Just as Job did many years before, Jeremiah curses the fact that he was even born. He's saying, "I hate my birthday!" He even goes so far as to say, "I not only hate my birthday, I hate the guy who burst out of the room with cigars saying, 'It's a boy!' I don't like him either."

This is a sloppy prayer. This is the kind of prayer that few people have the courage to pray before a holy God. But Jeremiah lifts it up, and note that it has been recorded in Scripture for our sake. God is not afraid of our honesty. He can handle authentic prayers lifted from the depth of our pain. As a matter of fact, he welcomes these prayers.

NEW TESTAMENT CONNECTION

Hang in There

The apostle Paul addresses the reality of facing suffering and hanging in there. He puts it this way:

> But we have this treasure in jars of clay to show that this all-surpassing power is from God and not from us. We are hard pressed on every side, but not crushed; perplexed, but not in despair; persecuted, but not abandoned; struck down, but not destroyed. We always carry around in our body the death of Jesus, so that the life of Jesus may also be revealed in our body. (2 Corinthians 4:7–10)

ILLUSTRATION | The Stories of Ordinary People

Jeremiah does what all of us can do. He hangs in there! He is bruised, battered, and discouraged, but he keeps his eyes on God. He expresses his sorrow and confusion, but he keeps on preaching. He is knocked down, but he gets up again.

Ordinary people can stand strong, even when it hurts. If you were to talk with a dozen followers of Christ who have stood fast during a hard time, through tears and suffering, you would find a common theme. Each one would tell you that they are glad they hung in there. They are thankful that they did not throw in the towel and quit. In the same way, if you ask those who have faced hard times in their faith and have caved in to pressure, they would tell you how much they regret it.

If you have stories of people you know, even members of your church, who have stood strong through hard times, you may want to tell their story—or perhaps better, let them tell their own story.

INTERPRETIVE INSIGHT | Hope in the Midst of Pain

Jeremiah teaches us another lesson as we look at his life. In his prayer recorded in chapter 20, he expresses deep pain and frustration. Yet, right in the middle of his prayer, we are surprised with these words:

> Sing to the LORD!
> Give praise to the LORD!
> He rescues the life of the needy
> from the hands of the wicked. (Jeremiah 20:13)

Where do these words come from? Jeremiah is experiencing the worst time of his life. He is pouring his heart out in a messy prayer, yet he starts praising God. What's up with that?

If we recall Jeremiah's call, we can hear God's promise expressed again. God had said to Jeremiah: "You must go to everyone I send you to and say whatever I command you. Do not be afraid of them, for I am with you and will rescue you" (Jeremiah 1:7–8). It seems as if Jeremiah is starting to understand that God has been with him, even in the hard times. We can almost hear Jeremiah say, "I guess God does rescue the life of the needy from the hands of the wicked." Jeremiah is saying, "I guess he has been with me. I'm still breathing. I'm still alive. I haven't been killed. Maybe it could have been worse." We get the sense that Jeremiah looks up from his pain and realizes that God has been with him. As a result, he lifts up words of praise.

INTERPRETIVE INSIGHT | Guarding Your Spirit

It's one thing to stay faithful to a hard assignment. It's another thing to stay sweet-spirited. When we are facing painful times, it is easy to become bitter and hard-hearted. Jeremiah is able to maintain a soft heart, even in hard times. After forty years of faithfulness, with no fruit to show for his efforts, he writes the book of Lamentations. He has warned the people for four decades, and now they are in exile. Jerusalem has been conquered, and the people are prisoners of war. Nevertheless, we hear Jeremiah lift up these words:

> Yet this I call to mind
> and therefore I have hope:
> Because of the LORD's great love we are not consumed,
> for his compassions never fail.
> They are new every morning;
> great is your faithfulness. (Lamentations 3:21–23)

Jeremiah's heart is still sensitive to God. He still sees beauty; he still sees grace. He still feels the tender hand of God. And he says, "Great is *your* faithfulness to *me*." It is one thing to see the grace and power of God when things are going well. But when a person has spent decades facing pain and struggle and that person can still celebrate the faithfulness and compassion of God, he or she is a true hero of faith.

SIGNIFICANT SCRIPTURE

Lamentations 3:21-26

NARRATIVE ON LIFE | Thankful for the Harvest

Jesus talks about how different people will see different harvests for the ministry they do. Some will see a harvest that is a hundred times what was sown, others a harvest that is sixty times, and others a harvest that is thirty times. We will never know why some people do their ministry and seem to have amazing harvests and others are just as faithful and they see very little results. This side of heaven we won't understand why. But what we can all do is enter into the joy of thankfulness whenever we see God bringing in a harvest.

All followers of Jesus should celebrate when they hear about a church where God is on the move. We should be thankful when ministries are growing and expanding. There is no room in the heart of a Christ-follower for petty competition with other churches or believers. The harvest God brings in is for his glory, and we need to be thankful for the harvest, even if it is happening across town or the world.

PAUSE FOR REFLECTION

Self-Examination Time

Some of those listening to this message will be feeling discouraged because they have made a terrible mistake somewhere along the way and quit on God's calling for their life. They need to be reminded that God's grace is big enough for them. They can make this moment a turning point.

Remind those gathered that God will graciously forgive them for any way they have failed to follow his plan for their life. Invite them to grab hold of the calling they once heard and to get back into the game. Assure them that the greatest joy they will ever know in the Christian life is to be rightly related to God through Jesus Christ and to be following the calling he has put on them, however painful. Allow a brief time of silence for people to reflect on their lives and to determine whether they are obeying God's call.

NARRATIVE ON LIFE | Ministry Even When It's Tough

There are some ministries that are especially challenging. These places of service demand a certain kind of person. Often, those who serve in these ministries do so with little praise or affirmation. Use this time to affirm those in your ministry and community who serve in these challenging places.

On the CD in your OTC kit, Bill Hybels talks about some of the ministries connected to Willow Creek that demand an enduring and faithful spirit:

- Special Friends (ministry to the mentally and physically challenged)
- Funeral ministry (ministries of compassion)
- Set-up and take-down of chairs (people with the ministry of helps)
- Parking attendants
- Nursery caregivers
- Children's ministry
- Work with the homeless
- And the list goes on

Identify some of the ministries connected to your church that demand hard work and get few praises. Then take some time to bless these people and let them know that God sees, God celebrates, and God will continue to empower them.

PAUSE FOR PRAYER

Meet Us Where We Are

Pray for people right where they are. Some possible prayer directions are:

- For those who are standing strong as they complete a hard assignment, lift up prayer for strength and for a sense of God's pleasure over their faithfulness.
- For those who have bailed out and are not fulfilling God's call, pray for grace and a renewed commitment to get back in the game.
- For those who are in a time of joy-filled harvest in ministry, pray to keep balance in their lives and for continued fruitful ministry.

NARRATIVE ON LIFE | Hard Assignments Still Exist

God expects all of his followers to be ready to take hard assignments and to be faithful all the way to the end. On the CD in the OTC kit, Bill Hybels tells stories of churches in Belfast, Ireland, and the Dominican Republic. These places face challenges that most congregations can't even dream of. You may want to use these stories, or you may use stories of your own about churches that are staying faithful in situations that seem hopeless. Their example of steadfastness can call us to live with greater faith and commitment to God, even when hard times come.

LIFE APPLICATION | Take Heart and Stand Strong

God has his reasons for giving certain people hard assignments. He doesn't do it capriciously. He doesn't do it in a cavalier fashion. He figures out who has strong shoulders and a steadfast heart, and he calls them to this needed ministry. He figures out who has the strength that is needed and then entrusts them with a hard assignment. When he does, he still says, "I will be with you and will help you."

If we are chosen for a hard assignment, we must remember that we are not the first to face this. Many Jeremiahs have gone before us. The Son of God is the ultimate example of someone who took a hard assignment given by the Father. It was painful, but he did it willingly.

If you find yourself walking the same path that has been traveled by Jeremiah, Jesus, and many others, stand strong. Pray a messy prayer. Share your grief with God. But don't bail out! Stay the course and know that one day you are going to meet the One who had the hardest assignment of all, and he finished it for your sake. Then, he will take your hand in his nail-scarred hands and bring you home. On that day, it will all be worth it.

It isn't what you wish to do, it's what you will do for God that transforms your life.
HENRIETTA C. MEARS

4. A Word for Those Who Don't Walk Jeremiah's Road—Seek Balance

NARRATIVE ON LIFE | A Word to Those Who Are Seeing a Harvest

Just as most followers of Christ will have times when they experience what it feels like to have a hard assignment, we will also have times when we see great results in ministry. There will be times when the harvest is coming in, God is moving in visible ways, and joy is flowing freely. In these times we need to give praise to God, but we must also be careful to maintain balance in our lives.

When we get an exciting, adrenaline-producing assignment, we need to be sure we don't let it push us out of balance. Ministry can become an addiction and wreck our lives if we let it get out of control. The key is to thank God for the work he is doing and enter into the ministry with all our strength, but be sure that we still take walks with a spouse, play with our kids, hang out with friends, have time for an occasional nap, and make space to be with God one-on-one.

PAUSE FOR PRAYER

A Prayer for Those with Tough Assignments

Pause and take time to pray for those who are walking the road of Jeremiah. Pray for strength to stand strong. Pray also for them to have eyes to see that God is with them, even when the road is hard.

LIFE APPLICATION | Slowing and Growing Your Soul

There is an inverse relationship between speed and the care of your soul. We can't nurture our souls and go deeper when our hair is on fire and we are living life with the speedometer pegged in the red. No one admires the scenery along the autobahn when they are in the passing lane, shifting into fifth gear and driving 125 miles per hour.

No matter how much fruit we are seeing grow in our lives and ministries, we still need to take time to slow down and grow our soul. This means we must develop a discipline of pulling away from the crowd and the busyness of life and make space to meet with God. We need to pray, listen to God, and feed on his Word. Maybe we need to start keeping a journal of prayers and personal reflections. No matter what we do in this time, we need to be consistent and intentional about unplugging on a regular basis and growing our soul.

CREATIVE MESSAGE IDEA

I Have Decided

You may want to close your message with the singing of the great hymn, "I Have Decided to Follow Jesus."

SESSION

8

The Life-Giving Power of Hope

2 KINGS 25:1-12; EZRA 1:1-4; JEREMIAH 29:1-23

The Heart of the MESSAGE

The term "hitting bottom" has become popularized when speaking of individuals who have come to their lowest point in life (often because of addictions) and finally have nowhere to look but up. The people of Israel hit their bottom when the Babylonians invaded and the nation went into exile. Earlier in 722 B.C. the northern kingdom had been invaded by Assyria and was conquered. In 586 B.C. Jerusalem, the capital of the southern kingdom, fell. Everything seemed hopeless.

Yet, out of the ashes of judgment, hope began to arise. Even as the exiles were being sent to Babylon, a message of hope was being proclaimed. God's judgment was not just punitive, it was meant to be redemptive. God's plan was to gather a faithful remnant and restore his people, after seventy years of exile.

Since this is the final message in the Old Testament Challenge series of sermons, we will take a whirlwind review of some of the key themes found in this entire course.

The Heart of the MESSENGER

God breathes hope. All through the Old Testament, even in the most painful and darkest moments of Israel's history, God loves and leads his people. From the harshest moments of judgment, we can hear the message of hope come through.

Take time as a leader to think through your own reading of the Old Testament. How have you seen God show up among his people and bring hope? How have you experienced God's hope filling your own life over these past weeks? How has a new hope in God and love for his Word grown in the life of your congregation? As you reflect on these hope-filled moments, celebrate God's goodness and let this spirit of confidence in God's power and love guide your teaching of this final session.

Also, since you will conclude with a review of some key lessons and messages from the Old Testament Challenge, be sure to review what God has said to you over these past thirty-two weeks. You can be confident that God has spoken to his people in powerful ways, and the review of these lessons will propel each person forward in a desire to grow in their relationship with God and with the community he has established among his people.

Brief Message OUTLINE

1. The Life-Giving Power of Hope
2. Celebrating Central Old Testament Lessons

- Lesson 1: There Is a God
- Lesson 2: Sin Leads to Death
- Lesson 3: God Longs for Covenant Relationship with His Children
- Lesson 4: God Has the Power and Desire to Deliver His Children
- Lesson 5: God Is Never in a Hurry; He Is More Concerned Who We Are Becoming Than When We Get There
- Lesson 6: God Will Use Whom God Will Use
- Lesson 7: God Is Holy and Calls His Children to Grow in Holiness
- Lesson 8: The Cycle of Sin Is Vicious
- Lesson 9: God Cares for the Suffering
- Lesson 10: God's Wisdom Will Transform Our Lives If We Let It
- Lesson 11: God Continues to Call Us Back to Himself

1. The Life-Giving Power of Hope

ILLUSTRATION | The Borg

In *Star Trek, the Next Generation*, there is a powerful image that parallels this concept of exile and assimilation into another culture. It is called "The Borg." The Borg is a huge spaceship that travels from culture to culture and takes over entire planets. When the people from the planet are conquered, they are plugged into the Borg, and their minds and any sense of individuality are snuffed out. They become part of a collective mind; they are assimilated.

This picture is similar to what happened when a nation went into exile. The goal of exile was not just to relocate the people; it was to remove all sense of national pride, love for a homeland, language, culture, or anything that would cause the people to long for home. The goal was to assimilate a whole culture and make it disappear.

WORD STUDY

Exile

Exile means forced relocation. It means you will leave your home forever. A superpower conquers a country and gives most of the population a choice: Move or die. This is how ancient superpowers made sure that people would not try to rebel and recapture their homeland. This happened to the northern kingdom in 722 B.C. and to the southern kingdom in 586 B.C.

For nations in those days, exile was the end. Humanly speaking, the idea of coming back to their homeland after a time of exile wasn't even an option. People who went into exile knew what to expect. They would eventually blend in with the other peoples of the ancient world, and their story, their culture, their language, and their faith would all disappear.

NARRATIVE ON LIFE | What If It Happened To You?

Imagine, for a moment, that you were forced to leave everything familiar. You have to leave your home and your country, and you must go live in a place that you don't know. You lose your job. You don't know the local language but are forced to learn it to survive. You don't know the customs. Everything is different.

Once you arrive as a prisoner of war in your new country, you realize that you will never have power in this place. You will never have influence. You have no resources, no wealth, and no means of attaining them. You are a stranger in a strange land. You will never belong. Your children will grow up with no connectedness to their national or religious roots except what you try to pass on to them. That's what it meant for Israel to live in exile. It looked like the end of the dream.

If this happened to us, how would we respond? Could we press on? How would our lives and our faith be challenged?

HISTORICAL CONTEXT | The Saddest Day in Israel's History

We all have certain moments in our personal history that are low points. This is also true of nations. For the people of God, one of the saddest moments came in 586 B.C., when Nebuchadnezzar and the armies of Babylon invaded Jerusalem and conquered it. They had come before and placed the people of Judah under their control, but they had always left the nation intact and someone on the throne. In 586 B.C. the Babylonians exiled the vast majority of people and destroyed the city. It was the saddest day in the history of Israel.

Earlier in 722 B.C. the Assyrians had conquered the northern kingdom. At that time, ten of the twelve tribes of God's people had ceased to exist. Then, in 586 B.C. the southern kingdom fell. This marked the end of Israel as a nation. They were no longer a united nation or a divided nation. They were no longer a political entity at all. They were dispersed among the Gentiles.

NARRATIVE ON THE TEXT | The Beginning of the End

SIGNIFICANT SCRIPTURE
2 Kings 25:1-12

In 2 Kings 25 we get a picture of how bad things got near the end of Judah's history. Babylon had become the dominant world power. Jeremiah, a prophet at that time, kept saying to people, "Exile is coming. Babylon will invade and conquer Jerusalem." But the people would not believe him. They were sure God would never let the holy city of Jerusalem fall under the sword of a foreign army.

Sadly, everything Jeremiah predicted came true. Zedekiah, one of the final kings of Judah, rebelled against the king of Babylon. As a punishment, Zedekiah's sons were murdered in front of him, and then his own eyes were gouged out so that this would be the last thing he ever saw. Nebuchadnezzar set the temple of God on fire, destroyed the palace and every important building in Jerusalem, and finally broke down the wall of the city. It was a complete and utter demolition of the capital of the nation of Judah and subjugation of all those with any political power.

Those not killed were exiled to Babylon. A handful of the poorest of the land were left to tend whatever part of the land that could be productive. Even this handful of people was under the hand of Babylon and had to pay tribute to the king.

NARRATIVE ON LIFE | The Heart of Jeremiah

SIGNIFICANT SCRIPTURE
Jeremiah 29:1-23

Jeremiah writes a letter to the exiles in Babylon. These are the very people he had warned year after year. They are the ones to whom he had come with God's call to repentance over and over. These are the people who had refused to listen to anything Jeremiah said.

Imagine for a moment that you are Jeremiah. You have preached the truth and your audience has turned on you. They laugh at you. They mock you. They don't believe you. They throw you into prison. They cart you off to Egypt. Then, exactly what you warned them about comes true. Now, you write a letter to the very people who mocked you all those years. What tone would your letter have? What would be the condition of your heart?

CREATIVE MESSAGE IDEA | A Picture of Exile

As an object lesson, have a portion of the people gathered with you for worship taken out of the place you are meeting. One or two rows of people should be enough to make the point. You will need to have ushers ready to take this group to a preassigned place. It would be ideal if those who are exiled can still see and hear the worship service while they are gone. Have someone ready to play some quiet, sad music as these people leave. Let these people know that they will be coming back, but for now they are exiled and will be escorted out.

Ask everyone who is staying to wave good-bye! Let everyone know that this should be a sad occasion.

For most of us, we would be filled with anger and perhaps even righteous indignation. For Jeremiah, his heart is still tender. Although he deals with the reality of judgment and exile, he also speaks of hope and restoration, and he gives practical advice about how to live in their new land. Jeremiah shows a level of tenderness that most of us would find unthinkable in this setting.

NARRATIVE ON THE TEXT | Praying for Babylon

In his letter to the exiles in Babylon, Jeremiah calls them to settle in. They should try to establish a normal life there. He wants them to build homes, plant gardens, get married, have children, and establish themselves in the new land. Beyond that, Jeremiah says:

> This is what the LORD Almighty, the God of Israel, says to all those I carried into exile from Jerusalem to Babylon: "Build houses and settle down; plant gardens and eat what they produce. Marry and have sons and daughters; find wives for your sons and give your daughters in marriage, so that they too may have sons and daughters. Increase in number there; do not decrease. Also, seek the peace and prosperity of the city to which I have carried you into exile. Pray to the LORD for it, because if it prospers, you too will prosper." (Jeremiah 29:4–7)

The whole idea seems counterintuitive. Why pray for Babylon? This is the nation who has conquered them. These are the people who have destroyed Jerusalem, their holy city. Babylon is the ever-present reminder that they are strangers in a strange land. But God calls them, through the prophet Jeremiah, to pray for the prosperity of Babylon!

Again, God is concerned about his people and who they are becoming. At the beginning of the Old Testament Challenge, when we studied the desert wanderings of Israel, we learned that God cared more about who his people were becoming than he did about how long it took them to arrive in the Promised Land. Now again we see that God is shaping his people. He intends to bring them back home, but he wants them to experience growth in their seventy years

SIGNIFICANT SCRIPTURE

Jeremiah 29:1–23; Ezra 1:1–4

CREATIVE MESSAGE IDEA

Checking In on the Exiles

At this point, check in with your exiles. If you have the capability, project them on a screen so everyone who is gathered can see them. If you don't have the ability to do this, at least pause to remind those gathered that those who were exiled are still off somewhere else in the building.

ON THE LIGHTER SIDE | "I Told You So!"

If we were in Jeremiah's shoes, what phrase do you think we might be tempted to use at the beginning of the letter to the people in exile? Jeremiah had been giving warnings for years, but they had ignored him! They had been given countless chances to repent and turn around, but they refused! Jeremiah spoke the truth again and again, only to be met with resistance, beatings, and rejection. After all of this, when judgment finally came and everything Jeremiah prophesied came to pass, what four words could Jeremiah have used to start his letter? Here is a little hint: The four words start with "I" and end with "so."

It would have been easy for Jeremiah to say, "I told you so!" But he did not.

of captivity. Jeremiah lets the people know that this captivity will not mean the end of their people, culture, and faith. In seventy years they will have another chance to realize God's dream of building a new community of people who love and follow him.

NARRATIVE ON THE TEXT | God's Hand in History

By every known law of human history, the people of Israel should have ceased to exist after 586 B.C. There is no way on earth the people of Israel should have survived, except for one thing: God chose that they would. God chose it.

Nebuchadnezzar died in 562 B.C., and Babylon went into rapid decline. It is invaded and defeated by a new kingdom—Persia. Cyrus, the king of Persia, decided on a new way to handle exiled people. Under the hand of God, he released the people and allowed them to go back to their homeland. In Ezra 1:1–4 we read:

> In the first year of Cyrus king of Persia, in order to fulfill the word of the LORD spoken by Jeremiah, the LORD moved the heart of Cyrus king of Persia to make a proclamation throughout his realm and to put it in writing:
>
> "This is what Cyrus king of Persia says: 'The LORD, the God of heaven, has given me all the kingdoms of the earth and he has appointed me to build a temple for him at Jerusalem in Judah. Anyone of his people among you—may his God be with him, and let him go up to Jerusalem in Judah and build the temple of the LORD, the God of Israel, the God who is in Jerusalem. And the people of any place where survivors may now be living are to provide him with silver and gold, with goods and livestock, and with freewill offerings for the temple of God in Jerusalem.'"

The behavior of Cyrus was unprecedented in the ancient world. His choice came because "the LORD moved [his] heart." What a reminder that God's hand is always active in human history. We don't know if Cyrus had any idea that God was working in his heart, but through his decisions, God spared his people and

NEW TESTAMENT CONNECTION

Pray for Those Who Persecute You

When God calls the people to pray for God's blessing on Babylon, this should be a familiar theme to followers of Christ. It was Jesus who said:

> You have heard that it was said, "Love your neighbor and hate your enemy." But I tell you: Love your enemies and pray for those who persecute you, that you may be sons of your Father in heaven. He causes his sun to rise on the evil and the good, and sends rain on the righteous and the unrighteous. (Matthew 5:43-45)

The heart of God, in both the Old and New Testaments, beats with love. He wants us, as his children, to operate with compassion and mercy, even toward those who have wronged us.

ON THE LIGHTER SIDE | Some Things We Have Never Heard Of

It is important to note that Jeremiah's promise that the people of Judah will one day be set free and return to Jerusalem would have seemed like a complete fantasy to the people. In those days, when a country was conquered and taken into captivity, they never returned. They ceased to exist as a nation. Think about all of the small countries that were once around Israel. What do you hear about them these days? How many of you have a neighbor who's a Moabite? Do you have a favorite Hittite restaurant in your neighborhood where you go occasionally to get some home-style Hittite cooking? Where was the last time you went to a concert and heard vintage music by the Three Edomite Tenors?

brought them home. On top of it all, Cyrus even did some fund-raising and helped gather resources so that the people of God could go back to Jerusalem and begin reconstruction of the city and the temple.

NARRATIVE ON THE TEXT | The Years of Rebuilding

When Israel comes home, they begin to rebuild the city. The rebuilding process takes a long time. The books of Ezra and Nehemiah cover more than a century and chronicle the rebuilding of the city, the temple, and the national and religious life of Israel.

But what gets rebuilt is not precisely what many of the people were hoping to see. Israel used to be a nation with millions of people. According to Ezra 2, only about 43,000 people come back. The city is not the grand and impressive place it was before. The temple never takes on the same majestic beauty it had in the days of Solomon. There is an excitement about being home, but there is a sense that something is missing.

All the old things the returned exiles had used to create a sense of identity are gone. They never have a son of David on a throne. They cannot govern themselves. They have no army. The walls of Jerusalem are in shambles. They are now an obscure, tiny group of people on a small piece of land somewhere in the massive Persian Empire.

NARRATIVE ON LIFE | A New Time and a New Dream

At one time Israel had dreams of impacting the world. Now they were a ragtag bunch of refugees who have been released from almost two generations of exile. What can they offer? What impact can they make? What difference can this tiny group of people really make?

Long ago Israel had hoped to become a superpower like Babylon or Assyria. By this time it has become painfully apparent that this dream will never happen. Israel will never see a mighty king lead them to win great battles, possess enormous wealth, and conquer new lands. These dreams are dead, and the people finally realize that these are the wrong dreams. They are foolish dreams. They aren't God's dreams for his people, and they never have been.

A few among them begin to dream a new dream. God births in them a new vision. They realize that what looks like the end could be a beginning. Maybe

CREATIVE MESSAGE IDEA | Welcoming the Exiles Home

The exiles come home after being away for decades. It is hard to imagine the emotion after such a long time lived in forced captivity. Against all odds, God acts and the exiles come home again. Imagine the joy.

At this time, invite the exiles from your congregation to come back. Play music that is joy-filled and energetic—something that fits the excitement of the moment. Use this moment to emphasize what a high point this is in the history of God's people.

they can finally become a community that will be great in the sight of God. Some begin to believe and understand that the greatness God wants to birth in them is not about armies, power, wealth, or things that make them look impressive in the eyes of the world. Greatness is to be based on turning their hearts toward God and humbly following him.

From the beginning God had a dream of building a new community of people who loved him, each other, and the world. Finally, it seems as if this dream is beginning to come alive in the hearts of God's people.

INTERPRETIVE INSIGHT | "Not My Will, But Yours Be Done"

From the very beginning of God's interaction with human beings, he was waiting for a little group of people who would be willing to form a community and say, "God, not our will but yours be done." He longed to see his followers live lives that declared, "We will die to all the stupid, foolish dreams of our lives. We will not long for and invest our lives in the pursuit of wealth, power, and success. We will long for your will, and your will alone."

The irony with Israel is that when they had a place of authority and power, they never used it to expand God's kingdom. When they had kings on the throne and military might, they seemed to become weaker and weaker. Now, with no formal government, no army, no wealth, most of their population gone, and no human authority at all, they have finally come to a place where God can use them. They are finally ready to say, "Not our will but yours be done!"

2. Celebrating Central Old Testament Lessons

With the time you have left, do a brief review of some of the key lessons learned in the OTC. Touch on these lessons, and other ones you feel your congregation should remember as you bring this journey to a close.

Lesson 1: There Is a God

We started the Old Testament Challenge with a fundamental lesson. There is a God. God exists eternally in trinitarian fellowship as Father, Son, and Holy Spirit. Out of this community, this trinitarian joy and delight, God creates. He does not do this because he is bored or because he is lonely. God does not create us so that

HISTORICAL CONTEXT | Map Time

If you look at a map we have of the Persian Empire at this time in history, you will see that it went from India all the way to Greece and from central Russia all the way down south to Libya. Within this expansive kingdom, the land now occupied by Israel was almost unnoticeable. It would have been easy for Israel to believe that they had nothing left to offer the world.

he will have little servants to do the chores he does not want to do. Rather, out of the magnificent richness of the eternal community experienced by the Trinity, God decides to broaden the circle. He longs to invite us to live in his love. This invitation is not for us to become little gods, but it is for us to bask in the glorious fellowship of the Trinity. God truly exists, and he invites us to enter into a relationship with him.

You will want to review Session 1 of Kit 1 in the OTC as you focus on the lesson about who God is and his plan for us to live in community.

NEW TESTAMENT CONNECTION

The Heart of Jesus

God wants all of his children to live with humble hearts. The more we yield to him, the more he can use us. Jesus is an example of complete humility and submission to the Father. It was Jesus who said: "My Father, if it is possible, may this cup be taken from me. Yet not as I will, but as you will" (Matthew 26:39).

As Jesus faced the cross, he affirmed his full submission to the Father by saying three times that he would not seek his own will but his Father's will. This same spirit must come alive in the lives of Christ's followers today if we are going to realize God's dream for our lives.

Lesson 2: Sin Leads to Death

God created men and women to live in community. But when the Fall came, sin entered the picture and community died. God's plan was for community. His desire was for human beings to live in harmonious and loving relationship with him and with each other. God did his part. He made us and gave us a wonderful place to meet with him and enter into rich and life-giving relationship with each other.

Sometimes the best of plans go bad. In chapters 3–11 of Genesis we see the downward spiral of sin. In this section of the Bible we see four distinct scenes: Adam and Eve, the story of Cain and Abel, the Flood, and the Tower of Babel. As we watch the drama unfold, we see things go from bad to worse. In these scenes we see sin go deep and spread wider. We also learn from God's response to the sinful choices made by his children.

You will want to review Session 2 of Kit 1 in the OTC as you focus on the lesson about the impact of sin.

Lesson 3: God Longs for Covenant Relationship with His Children

In the OTC we learned that God doesn't give up on his children. The primary expression of the faithful love of God is revealed in covenant. God is a covenant-making God, and he is the one who says, "I'll be with you."

In the ancient world there were two kinds of covenants. There were *bilateral* covenants between two equal partners, and there were *unilateral* covenants between a stronger and a weaker partner. The covenant between God and Abraham was clearly unilateral.

CREATIVE MESSAGE IDEA | Time to Celebrate

Pause at this point and take time to celebrate what God has been teaching your congregation through the Old Testament Challenge. Ask God to help you be a people that dream his dreams and experience his joy in deeper ways.

Respond by doing one or more of the following:

- Sing a song that expresses praise to God for his power and presence.
- Have someone share a testimony about how their dreams and longing for life have changed as you have gone through the Old Testament Challenge.
- Lift up a prayer asking God to help you as individuals and as a group to yield yourselves fully to his dreams and plans.

Generally speaking, in unilateral covenants, the stronger partner always had an agenda. The covenant was based on the idea that there was something the stronger partner could gain from the weaker partner. In Abraham's day, the stronger partner in a covenant was usually after water rights, land to graze his herds on, or something else that would benefit the stronger party in the agreement. Here is the key question we need to ask, "What does God get out of this relationship?" He knows the human race. He knows he will be facing heartache, ingratitude, folly, and sin. So what does he gain from this covenant? He gets someone to bless!

God gets someone on whom he can pour out all of the affection and warmth and mercy and love of his heart, even though it's going to break his heart. This is why the Old Testament writers are staggered by the fact that the God who created the heavens and the earth would choose to enter into a covenant with fallen human beings.

We also learned that God always had a sign that went with a covenant. The sign of Abraham's covenant was circumcision. This sign of the covenant was available to people who were not Hebrews. They too could be a part of the circumcised covenant people. Note that when God called Abraham to institute circumcision, Abraham obeyed that very day.

You will want to review Session 3 of Kit 1 in the OTC as you focus on the lesson about God and how he established covenant relationships with his people.

Lesson 4: God Has the Power and Desire to Deliver His Children

The people of Israel ended up in Egypt and were enslaved by Pharaoh. Out of this situation we learned another important lesson about God: He is a deliverer. He saw their oppression, came down, and called Moses to lead the people out of captivity. Moses was not excited about this assignment. He gave five objections, but God still called him. So, with trembling knees, Moses went to be part of God's delivering plan.

God did amazing things to deliver his people. He sends the many plagues, but Pharaoh remains stubborn. One of the shocking statements of Pharaoh came after the frog plague. There were frogs everywhere, but when Pharaoh asked Moses to get rid of them, Moses asked, "When do you want me to pray for God to send the frogs away?" Pharaoh's answer was almost comical, "Tomorrow. I think I can tolerate one more night with the frogs. I'd rather not have to do what God wants me to do. I think I can put it off another day."

Later God provides manna for the people. He shows that that not only is he their deliverer, but he will provide for them, one day at a time. Then they come to the Jordan River at flood stage and they learn the lesson of the first step. Sometimes God waits to act until we take a step of faith. All through this time in their history we learn that God has the power and the desire to deliver his people.

You will want to review Sessions 5 and 7 of Kit 1 and Session 1 of Kit 2 in the OTC as you focus on the lesson about God as deliverer.

Lesson 5: God Is Never in a Hurry; He Is More Concerned Who We Are Becoming Than When We Get There

There is a huge spiritual lesson in the travel plans God had for Israel: God is not in a hurry! God's primary concern is not speed. Ours usually is. But God knew that *where* the people of Israel were going was not nearly as important as *who* they were becoming. God knew that possessing a land flowing with milk and honey was not nearly as important as having a heart flowing with love, justice, courage, and faith. God's first concern was not how fast his people got to the Promised Land. His deepest concern was that they would be the right kind of people once they arrived. If it took forty years to prepare their hearts, then so be it!

You will want to review Session 7 of Kit 1 in the OTC as you focus on the lesson about God's timing.

Lesson 6: God Will Use Whom God Will Use

All through the Old Testament we discovered that God used surprising people to accomplish his purposes. God used humble midwives, Shiphrah and Puah, to protect the children of Israel. He called Gideon, Deborah, and other surprising people to lead as judges. David was the youngest in his family, but he became king. Elisha was a rich kid who gave it all up to follow Elijah and become a prophet. Amos was a farmer whom God called to preach to kings. Over and over through the Old Testament we see God using whomever he chooses to do his will.

There are examples of this lesson all through each of the four kits in the OTC.

Lesson 7: God Is Holy and Calls His Children to Grow in Holiness

God is perfectly holy. We are not. We are an unholy people desperately seeking a way to grow in holiness! How do impure people learn to walk in holiness? The answer is, we walk with a God who is holy, and he transforms us. First, he *makes us holy* through his cleansing power and grace. Second, he teaches us to *grow in holiness* as we learn to walk in his ways. The people of Israel learn that growing in holiness is a process that takes a lifetime. As a nation, they learn that the journey toward holiness carries over many generations and centuries.

You will want to review Sessions 6 and 9 of Kit 1 and the messages of the prophets from Kit 4 in the OTC as you focus on the lesson about God's holiness.

Lesson 8: The Cycle of Sin Is Vicious

There is a basic cycle that repeats itself twelve times in the book of Judges, and it shows up other places in the Old Testament. Over and over again the people of God went through this heartrending process, and it seems as if they did not have the ability to look back and learn from their past.

It began with a time of *peace*. The people experienced a time of peace and prosperity. Things were going great. People were seeking God. They held fast to God's plan, and there was a time of peace.

Then came a season of *complacency* when the hearts of the people began to grow cold. They got used to the goodness of what God had given them. As their hearts grew complacent, their eyes began to wander away from the one true God and toward the idols and false gods for the nations around them.

Eventually they began to compromise and *sin* entered in. Their sinful hearts led them to wicked actions and the people entered into idolatry. They began to enter into all kinds of immorality, the same kinds of immorality as the people who lived in that land.

Sin gave birth to *pain*. Most often the people of Israel experienced pain when the nations around them came in and invaded, attacked, and conquered their land. These invading people oppressed God's people and brought untold pain and sorrow into their lives.

This oppression could last for years or even decades. When the people hit a point of brokenness, they *cried out to God*, saying, "God, save us. Help us. Get us out of this situation."

Then God sent a *judge* to deliver his people. He raised up a leader who helped them fight off their oppressors. Over time, their enemies fled and the hearts of the people turned back to God—for a time.

Their victory led to a time of *peace*. But, after a time of peace the hearts of the people became complacent again. Over and over this cycle repeated itself.

You will want to review Sessions 3 and 4 of Kit 2 as you focus on the lesson of the downward spiral of sin.

Lesson 9: God Cares for the Suffering

In the book of Job we learned how God cares about those who suffer. Job's friends said what a lot of people still say, "If you're suffering, you deserve it. If you do good things, God will reward you. If you do bad things, you suffer." God was not pleased with their theology, and he still resists those who misrepresent him with this kind of teaching.

The real question in Job is, "Will Job still love God even if he doesn't shower him with good things?" Are human beings actually capable of love, or are we just reinforcement machines responding to God because he gives us stuff? There is a magnificent statement in Job that answers this question: "Though he slay me, yet will I hope in him" (Job 13:15).

Finally, at the end of the book, God appears. God asks Job all sorts of questions. God is not trying to show Job how ignorant he is. God is reminding Job how he loves all kinds of creatures, such as the wild ox and the ostrich, even though she is a forgetful mother. God loves them all even though they don't seem to be of any strategic value. It is simply God's nature to be gratuitous and loving.

By the end of the book Job cries out, "My ears had heard of you, but now my eyes have seen you [and that's enough]" (Job 42:5). God is seen to be a being of unspeakable goodness that notices and cares for the suffering of every human being. The suffering of Job and every other person matters more to God than we can imagine.

You will want to review Session 7 of Kit 3 as you focus on the lesson about suffering.

Lesson 10: God's Wisdom Will Transform Our Lives If We Let It

One rich area of learning came from studying Proverbs. Proverbs aren't laws, and they aren't promises; rather, there are catchy observations about the way things are most of the time.

Wisdom, which is such a key theme in the Old Testament, is not mostly about I.Q., it's about the ability to make right decisions. God longs for us to grow in wisdom and flee from folly.

You will want to review Sessions 5 and 6 of Kit 3 as you focus on the lesson about wisdom.

Lesson 11: God Continues to Call Us Back to Himself

The prophets of Israel became a voice for God—a conscience—that's unparalleled in human history. It is amazing to realize that the Bible makes so much space for all these prophets who were so strongly critical of God's people and their practices. We might think they would have tossed these books out, but they did not.

Elijah confronted a king, a queen, and a nation, and God revealed his power. Elisha left everything to take on the mantle of ministry and continued to be a voice of truth in a dark time of Israel's history. Amos held out a plumb line to show the people that their lives were not straight and true. He called God's people to feed the hungry, to care for the hurting, and to extend the love of God. Isaiah spoke to a generation who practiced religion but had hearts far from God, and he called them to a new and authentic faith. Hezekiah faced fear but chose to follow God even when his eyes could not see how God could deliver him. Micah called a whole generation to justice and righteousness. And, Jeremiah, through tears, beatings, and sorrow, continued to proclaim the word of the Lord. Through each of the prophets God is calling to his people, over and over. They remind us that the arms of God are always open, when we are ready to come home again.

You will want to review Sessions 1–7 of Kit 4 as you focus on the lessons from the prophets.

Wrap-Up

These are just a handful of the lessons you may want to review as you conclude the Old Testament Challenge. You may also want to close with a challenge for each person to begin a personal reading of the New Testament as a follow-up. It would be wonderful to have each person take a next step in their personal Bible study as they conclude the Old Testament Challenge. You might want to use some of the ideas in the *OTC Implementation Guide* to help encourage people to continue growing in their commitment to study and follow God's Word.